How to Publish Your Communication Research

❖ ❖ ❖

We dedicate this book to those people who
make the editor's job possible: unselfish,
insightful reviewers and authors who can get
past initial rejections to learn how to become
better writers and more successful scholars.

Steve Chaffee was the premiere example of a
reviewer, teacher, and scholar. Communication
lost an irreplaceable resource when Steve
passed away as this book went into production.
This book is a memorial to his unwavering
commitment to help others be better scholars.

❖ ❖ ❖

How to Publish Your Communication Research

An Insider's Guide

Edited by
Alison Alexander • W. James Potter

With Contributions by
James A. Anderson, Judee K. Burgoon, Steven Chaffee and Debra Lieberman,
Clifford G. Christians, Jean Folkerts, Thomas R. Lindlof, Alan M. Rubin

 Sage Publications
International Educational and Professional Publisher
Thousand Oaks ■ London ■ New Delhi

For information:

Sage Publications, Inc.
2455 Teller Road
Thousand Oaks, California 91320
E-mail: order@sagepub.com

SAGE Publications Ltd
1 Oliver's Yard
55 City Road
London EC1Y 1SP

SAGE Publications India Pvt Ltd
B-42, Panchsheel Enclave
Post Box 4109
New Delhi 110 017

Printed in the United States of America

Library of Congress Cataloging-in-Publication Data

How to publish your communication research: An insider's guide / edited by Alison Alexander and W. James Potter; with contributions by James A. Anderson . . . [et al.].
    p. cm.
Includes bibliographical references and index.
   ISBN 0-7619-2179-6 (cloth: alk. paper)
   ISBN 0-7619-2180-X (pbk.: alk. paper)
   1. Authorship—Marketing. 2. Academic writing. 3. Scholarly publishing. I. Alexander, Alison. II. Potter, W. James. III. Anderson, James A. (James Arthur), 1939-
   PN146.H69   2001
   070.5'2—dc21   2001003379

01 02 03 04 05 06 10 9 8 7 6 5 4 3 2 1

Acquiring Editor: Margaret H. Seawell
Editorial Assistants: Alicia Carter and Ester Marcelino
Production Editor: Claudia A. Hoffman
Typesetter/Designer: Janelle LeMaster
Indexer: Molly Hall
Cover Designer: Jane Quaney

Contents

❖ ❖ ❖

Preface

❖ ❖ ❖

Turning over your scholarship to the none-too-tender mercies of editors and reviewers is a frightening, humbling, and sometimes painful process. It can also be a very exhilarating and rewarding process—if you know what to do. This book is intended to help you experience the process in the most constructive manner so that it will bring more joy than pain.

The ultimate goal of this book is to help you make your scholarly work irresistible to editors and reviewers. We will do this by giving you lots of practical information that you cannot currently find in textbooks or even in many graduate programs. Much of the advice in this book might appear to be simple common sense. However, we can testify that almost all of this advice is not common at all—that is, it is not widely used, which is why almost all of the journals in our field routinely reject 80% or more of all manuscripts submitted for publication.

With so many manuscripts rejected for publication, can we conclude that the research is that bad? The answer is no. There are many good research studies that never see publication. The reason that so many manuscripts are rejected is that the writing is often not very good. There are many things that authors can do to improve their writing and thereby dramatically increase their chances of having their work accepted for publication in even the most selective of scholarly journals. Each chapter in this book will show you many things you can do to improve your writing.

We assume that you have already been thoroughly trained in theory, in methodology, and in the existing literature of our field. We also assume that you have identified an interesting question and an insightful method of probing the depths of that question. Maybe you have even written it up and presented it at a convention. Now you are ready to engage in that frightening task of preparing a manuscript for publication consideration.

In the first chapter, we outline the process of submission and show you how to avoid looking like an amateur. In Chapter 2, we show you that authors of any type of communication scholarship are in danger of falling into one (or all) of 10 traps. Knowing what these traps are will help you navigate through the manuscript writing process without getting caught in a fatal flaw.

Each of the remaining seven chapters focuses on a particular type of writing. These chapters are written by successful publishers of research. Cumulatively, these scholars have published several thousand research articles and book chapters. These people have all edited major communication journals and continue to serve on multiple editorial boards.

Chapter 3, written by Steven Chaffee and Debra Lieberman, describes how a literature review can introduce new research concepts, explicate existing concepts more clearly, advance theory, provide an overview of the current state of research in a field, and guide communication practitioners. In Chapter 4, Judee Burgoon focuses on steps in constructing and communicating theory, addressing the questions, Why is our field challenged for lacking theory and what can a beginning author do in that arena? Alan Rubin tackles the challenge of writing the quantitative study in Chapter 5. From providing an adequate rationale for an interesting question, to giving systematic information about the procedures used, to establishing the contribution to knowledge, Rubin charts the necessary components of the quantitative essay writing task.

Thomas Lindlof, in Chapter 6, overviews the special challenges of writing the qualitative study: explicating the action and discourse of the field and inviting readers to understand what it means to live in the scene under study. In Chapter 7, James Anderson focuses on one form of interpretive inquiry— empirical hermeneutics. How does one construct a narrative that displays particular interpretive claims? Anderson demonstrates this innovative technique. Clifford Christians, in Chapter 8, illuminates our understanding of writing within critical/cultural perspectives by presenting four major criteria used to evaluate such manuscripts. Finally, in Chapter 9, Jean Folkerts articulates major historical approaches and discusses the particular challenges of contextualizing time and place, applying a theoretical perspective and an appropriate method, all in the service of creating a spellbinding story.

—ALISON ALEXANDER
—W. JAMES POTTER

1

The Manuscript
Submission Process

Alison Alexander

❖ ❖ ❖

The focus of this chapter is on the process of taking that newly written work through the submission and publication process. What should you expect and what can you do to make the process easier?

❖ SELECT THE RIGHT PLACE
TO SEND YOUR MANUSCRIPT

First, find the right place for your manuscript. A good place to begin is the *Iowa Guide*, which provides information on over 100 communication journals and is updated about every two years. There you can find the name of the current editor as well as information about the journal focus, style requirements, and page length. Then, look through some issues of a journal in which you would like to publish. Notice what types of articles are published. Look at the topics, names of authors, types of writing styles, format, and use of graphics, tables, and photographs. Also, check carefully the review time and the publication lag. Again, the *Iowa Guide* provides this information, but more up-to-date information may be available in a yearly report published in the journal or available from the association that publishes it. Sometimes association newsletters will have useful information (e.g., that editor *X* has filled all remaining pages and requests that new articles be sent to upcoming editor *Y*). You should weigh exposure, review time, publication lag, and article appropriateness to select a journal for submission.

Journals publish information on required format and article length. Most journal articles tend to run between 20 and 30 typed pages. Although it may be difficult, try to keep your articles to the length prescribed by the journal. Pay particular attention to the instructions to authors, which are usually included in every issue, but are published at least yearly. Furthermore, remember to check with your colleagues; they can tell you things you cannot find in the *Iowa Guide* or in the journal's official editorial guidelines.

You will want to consider the prestige of a journal. Prestige is frequently correlated with the reputation of the professional association affiliated with the journal, as well as with the size of the journal's circulation, library subscriptions, and attentive readership. Certainly, publication in major journals of the field is a plus in the tenure and promotion arena. Nonetheless, regional journals, state journals, journals of smaller associations or divisions within associations, and even journals outside our field provide opportunities to speak to specific audiences.

Journal editors will sometimes include a statement defining their vision in the first issue published under their leadership. However, be aware that there is a simple and inescapable fact of publishing: like begets like. If a journal is known for its quantitative work, that is the kind of submission it will get. Somewhat like turning an ocean liner, changing a journal's profile is a slow process. For you, the hopeful author, there are two implications. First, the infrastructure and the predisposition are already there. If a journal is known for a certain kind of work, your work of the same kind will, one hopes, get a good and thorough review. If accepted, it will be read by individuals doing the same kind of work. Second, if you can discern that an editor is trying to steer the ship in your direction, you may get nurtured. However, be aware that the review process in this case can be unpredictable: Such a journal probably does not have a lot of experienced reviewers in this area, and reviews may contain unexpected comments. Also, even if the work is accepted, it may not be read by individuals working within your area.

Beyond where to submit, issues of *what* and *when* are important. One cardinal rule is to submit only to one journal at a time. Some even suggest that you should not submit a paper for review that is scheduled for presentation at an upcoming convention. That is too strict by our standards, but the published paper should not come out before the convention. Of course, everyone knows that you cannot publish the same paper twice. Prior publication of earlier versions or studies from the same data set must be revealed to the editor and will become a matter of editorial judgment. Manuscripts that have been published in whole or in substantial part elsewhere should not be submitted.

We encourage you to be certain that any work submitted is prepared to the best of your ability. Given the amount of voluntary time that reviewers spend with manuscripts, do not send in material that is not ready for rigorous review. To all you perfectionists out there, this does not mean wait another six months until you have rewritten four more times. It does mean that anyone should avoid pulling an all-nighter to finish a graduate term paper and then submit the paper to the journal to "just see what they think."

One secret: journals are expensive. In some fields, although not yet in our own, journals require a submission fee to offset the cost of the review process (this may mean that reviewers receive a small amount of money for their reviews). The author instructions will inform you if this is required. Also, some very few journals have a publication fee. Authors are charged per page for the costs of publication. You need to be aware of these possibilities.

❖ SEND IT TO THE EDITOR

When you have found the right place to submit your work, again examine the instructions to authors. Carefully read the policies and procedures. Also, review one final time the purview of that journal. Be sure to make a copy for yourself of whatever you send out for review. This last item becomes crucial in the era of word processing: A hard copy tells you exactly which of the versions cluttering your hard drive actually was sent out for review.

Send a cover letter with your submission, including all numbers and addresses for correspondence, particularly e-mail. Also, include the presentation history of this work: convention presentations of this or related work; related publications—particularly if this comes from the same data collection procedure; and any funding. In short, include anything that you would not want the editor to be surprised to learn.

A word of caution on format: Changing the format of a paper to match that required by a journal can be a real pain. So, why not send it in another format and change later if they are interested? Certainly, as editors we have never refused to review a paper because it was in the incorrect format. Some of our reviewers, however, have been less obliging. Mostly, they conclude that the work has been rejected elsewhere. It is your choice whether to change the format or not, but note that it can only be a negative in the evaluation process. You cannot know how much of a negative—and that is a big risk to take.

Much of this advice is common sense, but, amazingly, many manuscripts end up on an editor's desk missing vital sections. Table 1.1 will help you to check your manuscript before mailing. Table 1.2 details many common errors, oversights, and omissions.

❖ WHAT THE EDITOR WILL DO

When the journal office receives your manuscript, it will generally be given a number and stamped with a "received on" date. Then, the editor will take a careful look at the work. He or she may return the manuscript if it is not appropriate. A surprising number of articles are returned without review, depending on the editor. Most are returned because they are deemed incompatible with the journal's mission. As editors, we were sometimes quite puzzled why an author would think that a particular subject would be of interest to our journal. For instance, sometimes individuals will send an article to a mass communication journal if television is used in any way in an experimental manipulation, even if the research question and the literature reviewed have nothing to do with our discipline. A much smaller number may be judged by the editor as inadequately developed for the journal. An editor quickly learns not to waste

TABLE 1.1   Author's Checklist for Manuscript Submission

✔ Cover Letter
   Include a statement that the manuscript has not been previously published and is not
      under consideration elsewhere
   Provide a history of its presentation
   Acknowledge any funding

✔ Title Page
   Include author name(s), address, affiliation, e-mail address, and telephone number

✔ Abstract
   Title and abstract of requested length

✔ Text
   Full title on first page only
   Running head on all pages
   Author name not included

✔ References
   All authors referenced in text

✔ Tables
   Separate from text
   Tables titled and numbered
   Every table column has a heading
   Abbreviations explained

✔ Other
   Author notes, appendices, figures

Common Errors, Omissions, and Oversights

✔ Is the paper double spaced?

✔ Are copies all readable and checked for missing pages or lines?

✔ Does the length exceed the guidelines?

✔ Is the manuscript format the one specified in the guidelines?

✔ Are all pages numbered sequentially, starting with the title page?

✔ Is the article free of spelling and grammatical errors?

✔ Are the levels of headings within the text consistent and do they accurately reflect the
   article's organization?

✔ Are page numbers provided for all quotations?

✔ Do text and reference list agree both in terms of dates and spelling?

✔ Are the required number of copies and/or disks enclosed?

✔ Is the disk labeled with manuscript file name and the word processing software used to
   create the file (e.g., Word, WordPerfect, ASCII, etc.)?

✔ Is the journal editor's name and address current?

---

reviewers' time sending out work so poorly done that it will obviously be rejected. This is the crucial first step in editorial judgment.

If a paper seems acceptable and within the purview of the journal's mission, it will be sent out to two or three reviewers chosen for their expertise in the paper's content or methodology. At this point, you, the author, should receive an editor acknowledgment of manuscript submission in which you will probably be told both the assigned manuscript number and how long the review process should take.

A few more words on reviewer selection. How do editors select reviewers? Generally, one or two reviewers will come from the journal's editorial board. The editor knows their interests and areas, and will select based on that knowledge. This method, however, does not always work out. Let us just say that you find out that your friend, the foremost expert in nonverbal communication who is on that editorial board, did not receive your nonverbal paper to review. Prejudice? Sabotage? Probably not. Editorial board members are almost always pressed to review numerous papers, yet the editor also promises when at the time of appointment to the board to keep the reviewing to some acceptable level. So, your friend may just have received a new manuscript, as well as two other unexpected manuscripts earlier sent back to their authors for revision and resubmission, when your submission flew in over the transom. Voilà! Another reviewer is assigned. It happens . . . a lot. Oh, and by the way, if the reviewer suspects that a particular work is done by friends, close colleagues, or current or former students, that reviewer will return the manuscript for someone else to review.

What about the non–board members who may be asked to review your work? For an idea about who else is being asked to review manuscripts for this journal, look at the journal pages that, typically once a year, thank reviewers who are not on the board. Editors keep files or lists of potential reviewers with their areas of expertise, but frequently will look at references used within your work for ideas about who might be a good reviewer. Note, however, that you can ask in you submission cover letter that certain individuals *not* be asked to review your work because of deep theoretical differences. You can even suggest reviewers, although whether they are accepted or not will vary by editor and by circumstances. We suggest that you keep such requests to a minimum. In our discipline, most reviews are done in a double-blind process: Personal identification is stripped from the manuscript, which is then assigned a number; reviewers, too, are assigned a reviewer number. Neither author nor reviewer knows the identity of the other . . . in theory. In practice, it works better than you might think. We were always amused when someone excused himself or herself from a review because he or she knew the author—and they were wrong. It happens! It is not always possible to mask the identity of an author because of the small number of people working in an area. It is frequently hard to guess, however, whether the work is that of the established author or of a student.

❖ WHAT WILL THE REVIEWER DO?

Typically, within a week of receiving your manuscript, the editor will send your manuscript to the reviewers with a request to review it and return their comments by a due date, which is often about four weeks later. As you start adding up the time required for editor evaluation, mailing, and review, you are already at five weeks—and that is if everything goes smoothly. If the review is not received by the editor within that deadline, usually reminders will go out within a week or so to hasten the return of the review.

Two to three reviewers are the norm. Each will provide a review that usually runs one to two pages in length on average, and rarely more than three. Almost all reviewers will address the importance of your work, considering whether or not it includes significant questions that are explored in a methodologically sound manner and that contribute to the knowledge in our field. Thus, reviewers will address the nature of your question, how you have linked it to the existing theory and literature, the method and analysis of the study, and your interpretation of results. These are the dreaded "So what?" questions: Is this an interesting and important question? Does this work add to the existing knowledge in the field? Is the research well done? Does the work *communicate* these things to the reading audience?

Reviews come in at least three types: reviews that tell you what is wrong, reviews that tell you what is wrong and how to fix it, and reviews that tell you to do something else. Believe it or not, all have their pros and cons. Reviews that tell you what is wrong give you, the author, the maximal flexibility to fix the problems; however, they give you little guidance if this is a thorny problem with which you have wrestled before. Nor do they give you any hints as to what would be acceptable to that reviewer.

Reviews that tell you what is wrong and how to fix it include helpful hints to correct the problems identified. Again, this can be useful, but it can have the effect of limiting your options. If the reviewer suggests you examine research article X or literature Y, how will the reviewer respond if you decide against that suggestion? Alternatively, others can sometimes see holes and how to fill them much better than the author can. And, such suggestions give you ideas as to how to proceed with the revision. Finally, some reviews tell you to do something else. The most egregious of these reviews fail to deal with your work at all, turning in favor to the reviewer's vision of how this research question should be explored. These reviews are mostly ignored, because they provide no useful information to either the editor or the author. Sometimes, the author will not even see them. Upon occasion, however, this type of review does point to fatal flaws in the approach, which really was inappropriate for the problem identified. Sometimes, the reviewer will point to a mismatch between literature and method, which can be remedied by reframing the research study.

When completed, reviewers will send their recommendation to the editor, frequently with a cover sheet provided by the editor that asks them to check the appropriate category of *major revision, minor revision,* and *reject,* or other such categories. A space for confidential comments is often included.

❖   ALMOST DONE: BACK TO THE EDITOR

Reviewers provide the reviews, but the decision to accept, reject, or ask for revision is the responsibility of the editor (or in some cases the associate editor). The editor's decision may differ from the recommendation of any or all reviewers. Often, the reviewers may themselves disagree on whether to revise or reject. Sometimes, you, the author, will not know what any given reviewer has recommended to the editor.

When all the reviews are received, the editor will write you a letter advising you whether the work has been accepted, needs a revision, or is rejected. Copies of the reviews will be attached. If the paper is to be revised, the editor will give you a due date. Most journals try to return reviews within three months. If not notified within that time, the author may appropriately contact the editor for information.

❖ REVISION OR REJECTION?

When you receive the evaluation, the editor will have accepted, rejected, or asked for a revision of the manuscript. Just get it into your head that it will not be an unconditional acceptance—never! I was recently talking to an excellent reviewer who commented that for the first time in 20 years he was going to suggest acceptance on the first reading of a manuscript. This should give you some indication of how rare that phenomenon is.

What you must hope for is a request to revise and resubmit. Remember —R & R is good. Most manuscripts need to be revised, and many need to be revised more than once. Editors share a common amazement at how many manuscripts selected for R & R are never returned for the second round of reviews. Do not allow the review to intimidate and delay you. When you receive a revise-and-resubmit request, you have made a giant step forward in the publication process.

Variability within revise-and-resubmit requests are extensive, ranging from "We really like this; make these few changes and get this back" to "There may be something here; we can't really tell, but if you rewrite we'll take another look." This variety is compounded by differences in editor letters. Some are quite extensive, asking for specific responses to the editor's concerns. Others just ask you to respond to the reviewers' comments, without giving you any particular guidance. The latter gives you maximal freedom, the former maximal guidance. Because the editor is the final arbiter, knowing his or her take on what needs to be done can be quite helpful. Consider the reviewers' and editor's proposals carefully and dispassionately, and carry out the revisions or seek compromise solutions where you strongly disagree. Ideally, you would hope to be sure that you and the editor are clear on the revisions to be undertaken. Realistically, the revision process is one of negotiation. When resubmitting a revised manuscript, authors should enclose an extensive cover letter responding (politely) to all the reviewers comments and detailing what the author has done or not done to deal with those comments. Generally speaking, unless the revisions suggested are very minor, this revised manuscript and your cover letter will go back to the same reviewers. By that time, the reviewers should also have copies of the other reviews and the letter sent by the editor to you, the manuscript author.

Be aware that although a request to revise and resubmit is important, it does not guarantee acceptance. Revisions may reveal basic flaws that were not apparent in the original manuscript.

Unfortunately, letters from editors will generally be a rejection. With most journals working with a less than 15% acceptance rate, most manuscripts are rejected. Read the letter over, then go do something cathartic (and nonviolent). Beware of assumptions that might creep into your head. Good papers *do* get rejected. There is a litany of famous and successful books that were rejected by multiple editors before being accepted and becoming a success. Papers that get rejected at one journal are often accepted at another.

Remember that we began this book with the assumptions that you are thoroughly trained in our field and that you have identified and carefully written up your work. Now it is your job to rewrite and resubmit. Learn what you can from the reviews and carefully consider any mistakes you might have made. If the reviewers have identified a fatal flaw, then learn from your mistake and move on to other work. But what you will probably discover is that you have not adequately communicated your ideas to your reader. Sometimes you know your own arguments so well that it is very hard to see where you have not stated them clearly. Give yourself a deadline (we advise not more than three months) in which to complete the rewrite and send this work off to a different journal.

❖ ACCEPTANCE

Finally, your manuscript has been accepted. Frequently that news will come with a request for minor changes (perhaps to update a reference or fix some format errors). Although not a time to delay, this is the time to do a final careful reading for style or format errors, for careful phrasing, and for other details. Do all the things that you have put off to make this manuscript perfect. This is your last chance to do it easily. Most editors publish articles in the order of their receipt. They may delay for specific reasons, including assembling issues on related topics, or they may advance publication of an article for reasons of timeliness. Also, number of pages can become a factor in creating an issue with the most economical number of pages as determined by printing requirements.

Either the journal editor or a copy editor will read your final manuscript. Not only will this editor mark the manuscript with codes for the typesetter, he or she will note any errors that you may have made. No matter how clean you have made your work, you will be amazed at what an editor will find. In general, these are individuals with considerable experience, and we suggest you be guided by their suggestions. You will see the copyedited manuscript, and again it is important that you examine it carefully. This is past the time to make major revisions, but you must be sure that copyedited suggestions are appropriate.

The copyedited manuscript is then "set" for type. That is, either the computer file is manipulated to produce camera-ready copy or the paper is typed into a computer by a computer-entry typist. The author will receive these *galleys* for final proofing. Any alterations during the galley stage are extremely expensive, and can be charged to the author. The only alterations in the manuscript at this point should be ones that result from computer-entry error.

At some point in this process, you will be mailed a copyright form and a reprint order form. Typically, copyright is assigned to the journal. Look at the agreement carefully to understand its stipulations. After the journal is published, you will generally receive a small number of reprints and one or two complementary issues of the full journal.

At last, your article appears in print. Enjoy, because you have worked through a very complex submission and publication process to present your contribution to the knowledge of our discipline. Congratulations!

2

Avoiding Writing Traps

W. James Potter

❖ ❖ ❖

S cholarly journals do not publish research; they publish manuscripts. When trying to get our research published, one of the most common mistakes we make is to focus all our effort on research tasks and think little about the task of writing. We believe that if we do good research, the writing about it will not present any problems.

Many of us are excellent researchers, but we have great difficulty getting published because we do not know enough about writing. We are left to learn the skills of scholarly writing on our own. It is unfortunate that in graduate school the focus of our education is almost exclusively on research, with curricula composed of courses in theory, methods, and tool skills that will help us conduct research. We almost never receive instruction in writing. Instead, we learn the writing part of publishing in the School of Hard Knocks. The review process is very hard on us if we do not communicate our research well. There must be a better way than learning through rejection. There is. In this chapter we present 10 writing traps. If you are able to avoid these traps, you will be able to write much stronger scholarly manuscripts. And if your research is solid, your increased knowledge about writing will dramatically increase your chances of getting published.

❖   TRAP 1: WRITING A MYSTERY

Avoid writing a mystery: Tell the reader "whodunit" up front. Editors and reviewers do not read your manuscript to be entertained. They are not looking for a suspenseful narrative where all is revealed in an emotional climax on the last page of your manuscript. Instead, editors and reviewers read your manuscript to learn something of value about communication. You need to tell them what this something of value is very early in your manuscript.

This does not mean that you must tell the reader everything in the first paragraph. If you can do that, there is no need to write the rest of the manuscript. What this *does* mean is that you need to set the perimeter and the focus in the first few paragraphs. Setting the perimeter tells readers what you will not deal with in your manuscript. This limits readers' expectations so they do not ask you to deal with questions, concepts, and procedures that you regard as outside the bounds of your study. How do you set the perimeter? You cannot possibly, of course, list all the things your study will *not* address. So what do you do? The answer to this question is to avoid what you should *not* do. You should not introduce important concepts or terms unless you plan to deal with them fully in your manuscript. In short, do not create expectations about ideas that you are not addressing with the research. When setting expectations, remember that the first page is the most important; that on the first page, the first paragraph is the most important; and that in the first paragraph, the first sentence is the most important.

Setting the focus tells the readers what is most essential conceptually and methodologically. As for conceptual focus, funnel the reader's attention into one central question or one guiding theory that structures your inquiry. Methodologically, signal clearly to the reader whether you are taking a quantitative or a qualitative approach and which type of method you have used.

Mysteries are fun to read. We keep turning the pages in order to get clues to help us guess "whodunit." Authors of mysteries depend on curiosity to drive readers through the story. But in a scholarly manuscript, editors and reviewers want to arrive at useful insights of which they are confident. In order to achieve that confidence, reviewers skeptically examine each step in your decision making. Therefore, readers need authors to lay out a clear path and persuade them of the soundness of reasoning for each decision along the research path. Surprises are problems, so be clear and complete.

❖ TRAP 2: LOSING FOCUS

Do not lose the focus on your main argument. In the simplest sense, this means that you should avoid tangents. Cut out all material that does not contribute to the flow of your primary argument. Doing this, however, is much more than simply avoiding irrelevant material. It means avoiding the appearance of taking readers on tangents. This is very difficult to do, because writing requires a linear presentation. That is, readers encounter one word at a time, one sentence at a time.

At many points in our manuscript, we will run into an element-context problem. This is when we realize that readers cannot understand a particular element until they first see the context. However, to grasp the context, readers first have to understand the individual elements. As writers, we frequently feel the pressure to elucidate an element while at the same time keeping the reader's perspective on the bigger picture. How can we do this with the linear process of writing? It is very challenging, but it can be done. Before writing each paragraph, ask yourself what readers need to know at this point in your manuscript. Do not get upset if your narrative is not following the chronological order in which you designed and conducted the study. You are not writing a diary account of your activities to remind yourself of the order in which things occurred. Instead, you are attempting to create a picture in readers' minds that you have conducted research that makes a major contribution to how we think about some phenomenon of interest to them.

It helps to write in an obvious format that readers recognize. Use clear headings and subheadings for sections. Present internal summaries and transitions in key places. Start each paragraph with a good topic sentence, and then develop your idea in the paragraph's remaining sentences by presenting supporting examples as well as the particulars of your argument.

❖ TRAP 3: WRITING A 3 × 5 CARD
REVIEW OF THE LITERATURE

When we are preparing our review of the literature, many of us write an abstract of each relevant article on a 3 × 5 card. When we finish reading the literature, we have a stack of cards that describes the relevant studies forming the foundation for our research. This is a useful step, but it is a mistake to think that the pile of cards is the review of the literature. It is a trap simply to type up the information in your cards, one study after another, and use this series of abstracts as your literature review.

The purpose of the literature review is not to demonstrate to reviewers that we have done the required reading. The purpose is to construct a strong foundation for our decisions. Thus, the literature review needs to be analytical and critical.

In order to write an analytical review, you need to break each study down into meaningful components. The typical components are purpose, methods, analyses, and findings. These components can be broken down further. For example, the methods component of a quantitative study has the subcomponents of sample, measures, treatments, and procedures. Your literature review should then be organized by these meaningful topics.

It is also important to be critical in the review of the literature. This requirement can be intimidating to researchers, especially those beginning their publishing careers. You may think that criticizing the work of major theorists and established researchers is not a wise thing to do, because many of these scholars will be reviewers of your manuscript; however, being critical does not mean attacking a person or trying to invalidate his or her work. If the research you are critiquing has been published, then it is of a relatively high quality. However, no research study is perfect; all have flaws and limitations.

Being critical means that you need to make judgments of the value of previous research as a foundation for what you have done in your study. There is value in all published work, but there is also a limitation in every published piece. In the literature review, it is your task to show how other researchers have made decisions, and then to persuade readers that the decisions you made in your research conform to the best decision making that came before you. In short, you need to evaluate the literature critically to demonstrate that your study is in fact on the cutting edge and needed, that the evidence you use in your study is the best in this research tradition, and that the analyses you use are the strongest and most appropriate.

❖ TRAP 4: WRITING FUZZY HYPOTHESES

If you use a hypothesis-driven analysis, then write real hypotheses. Hypotheses are not loose guesses about what you might or might not find in your study. Instead, hypotheses should be carefully crafted predictions about what you should expect to find, given your review of the literature.

There are typically two traps that prevent scholars from presenting good hypotheses. One trap is the feeling that hypotheses should be written at a very general level; that is, authors fail to show the careful operationalization from a theoretical proposition into a testable statement. Oftentimes, authors will simply use the theoretical proposition as the hypothesis. When hypotheses are too general, it is difficult for readers to see a connection between the key terms in the hypotheses and how those concepts will be measured. Thus, authors need to specify how a construct is being operationalized. Is a construct represented in the test by one measure? If so, which one? Or is the construct an amalgam of several measures? If so, which measures, and how are those measures to be assembled into an aggregate scale to represent the construct? In making these operational connections between constructs and measures, it becomes important for the author to argue for the validity, reliability, and usefulness of those measures.

A second trap is the tendency to fail to specify the predicted relationships among the constructs. Typically, authors simply state, "There will be a relationship between X and Y." This tells readers nothing about the expectation for the strength or direction of the relationship. As for strength, authors often seem to act as if a statistically significant relationship is enough to argue that the strength of the relationship is meaningful. This is a flaw. Confusing the difference between statistical significance and substantive significance is a mistake that tells reviewers that the authors do not have a proper understanding of statistics, and that perhaps the authors also lack an understanding of the other claims they make.

❖ TRAP 5: THE BLACK BOX ANALYSIS

Sometimes, researchers will be so elliptical in describing their evidence-gathering and analyses methods that the reader is left in the dark. It is as if the results magically appear out of a secret process—a black box. Remember, editors and reviewers read your work with skepticism. In your analysis section, they want to be assured that you have employed the full power of your tests and that you have not violated any of the assumptions underlying those tests. You need to provide enough detail to convince reviewers that you are fully aware of your analytical procedures and that you have used them well.

When your results provide dramatic support for your hypotheses, reviewers want to believe that you have found something important. However, they need to be convinced that your measures are reliable and valid. In contrast, when your results are inconclusive, reviewers want to help you sharpen your analysis in order to give you a better chance of producing more conclusive results. But reviewers cannot help much with this task if authors do not provide much detail about their analyses.

❖ TRAP 6: JARGON

Scholarly research is focused on important ideas, and we refer to these ideas by using special terms. There are three types of terms: primitive, technical, and jargon. Primitive terms are those we use in a manner common to all readers. They do not require us to provide a definition in our manuscript. Examples in this chapter include such terms as *author, editor, reviewers, publication,* and *findings.*

Technical terms are words used to label constructs that have a precise and different meaning from alternative words that might seem to be synonyms. When you use technical terms, do not assume that all readers will completely understand your meaning for them. Clearly define these terms, and do so in a way that shows the reader what is special about your meaning. Examples of technical terms in this chapter include *review of the literature* and *hypothesis.*

Jargon is the use of a new and/or complicated phrase in place of a commonly accepted term that carries the same meaning. Using long or complicated terms when short words will do is showing off. The use of jargon increases the barriers to communication and should be avoided.

Go through your manuscript and circle your key terms. Are you using the commonly held meaning for those terms you are treating as primitive? Have you carefully explicated your technical terms? If you find a term that looks like jargon, find a synonym. If you cannot find a synonym, ask yourself why you are using that term, then either drop it or turn it into a technical term.

❖ TRAP 7: ATTEMPTING TO HIDE THE FLAWS

Be honest. Do not ignore your study's flaws and hope that the reviewers and editor will not notice. The review process is designed to identify the flaws in your research and then to render a judgment about the severity of those flaws and whether they can be fixed in a revision or not. Ignoring the flaws makes the reviewers infer that you are not a good enough scholar to perceive them or understand their implications. These inferences are likely to lead to a recommendation for rejection, because the reviewers reason that you may not be capable of undertaking a suitable revision. Instead, it is better for you to acknowledge the flaws at appropriate places in your manuscript. However, be careful not to overdo this and leave the reader with the impression that you are convinced your study is worthless.

All studies have flaws, so do not think that you cannot get your work published unless it is perfect. Do not let yourself become neurotic because you have never been able to execute the perfect study.

❖ TRAP 8: FIXATING ON PROBLEMS

Turn problems into opportunities. We all do this in our reviews of the literature. We cite previous work as being flawed in some way, and use this problem in the literature as an opportunity for our current study. Doing this provides a good foundation for our study. Consider following this same strategy within your own study. When you find an apparent shortcoming in your own research, think about how you can turn that weakness into a strength. For example, let us say you are conducting a study about how Americans want a wide diversity of types of entertainment on television. You gathered data and find support for your claim of viewer diversity. Your sample, however, is 400 college sophomores. How can you generalize from college sophomores to all Americans? You cannot. This is a weakness of your study. How can you turn this weakness into a strength? You could point out from past research that college students expose themselves to less television than other adults and that the college audience is more homogeneous in its preferences than are other age groups; therefore, if we find any diversity in this relatively homogenous group that watches relatively little television, we should then expect at least as much diversity in the American population.

❖ TRAP 9: FORGETTING ABOUT THE READER

Put the reader inside the topic of your manuscript. Too often, scholarly writers take the stance that the facts speak for themselves. But the facts do not speak at all: We have to speak for them. We write the manuscripts; they do not write themselves.

Writing well means bringing the reader into your world. You can achieve this by making your topic vivid and exciting. Show rather than tell. Show the reader the controversy. Show the implications of your findings.

There are some techniques good writers use to give readers easy access to their worlds. One technique is to raise questions where you think the reader would be asking questions. As you answer a question, show how that raises another question, and so on. This pulls the reader through the analysis of difficult material. Use short sentences where possible. Cut out extra words. Use an active voice.

❖ TRAP 10: LETTING NEGATIVE EMOTIONS DESTROY YOUR EFFORT

By the time we send a manuscript to a journal for publication consideration, we have a great deal of ourselves invested in the project. Our future as a scholar may also be invested in the publication decision. If our manuscript gets accepted, we may get a raise, a promotion, or even tenure. Therefore, opening the decision letter from a journal editor is most often an extremely emotional event. If the letter is one of acceptance, we are elated. The heart beats faster and the head swells several sizes! But if the manuscript is rejected, we feel frustrated and even angry.

Learn to use your emotions as motivators. This is easy to do when we feel happy and successful: Positive reinforcement is a powerful motivator. However, anger can also be a powerful motivator if you know how to harness it constructively. Tell yourself that the reviewers were wrong and that you can clarify your arguments to a point where you will show them that your study is one of the best ever done.

When we use our emotions—even negative ones—as motivators to improve the manuscript, we keep learning. Eventually the manuscript may get published in a more appropriate journal or one with less rigorous publication standards. More important, however, when we keep learning, we get better and the next study we do will be of higher quality and more likely to be successful in the review process.

❖ CONCLUSION

The value of scholarly writing is judged by how well it is able to put the author's ideas into the minds of readers. Your writing is the bridge from your study to the readers' needs and experiences. Your first draft is usually not much of a bridge, because you are focused almost exclusively on the study itself. A first draft serves as a faithful diary of your thinking in the research process. This is an essential beginning, but it is only a first step. Be prepared to rewrite.

The communicative quality of your manuscript can only be improved through rewriting. Show your work to your colleagues and ask for honest evaluations. You will be surprised at how much you can learn about your own work by listening to people who know far less about your research than you do. As you get feedback from colleagues, you will understand much more about how your readers encounter your ideas. With repeated rewriting, you extend the bridge. Rewriting is hard work, but it is the only way to keep extending the bridge until eventually your work not only is published, but also affects the way your readers regard your topic—and you.

3

The Challenge of
Writing the Literature Review
Synthesizing Research for Theory and Practice

Steven Chaffee
Debra Lieberman

❖ ❖ ❖

Many advances in empirical knowledge about communication come via literature reviews that synthesize a large number of studies into a coherent view. A review can take many forms, one being the familiar review within a study. A thorough research report proceeds from a review of prior related work, explains how the present study addresses an issue within that literature, and concludes with an analysis of how the new findings alter the picture. So each investigation begins—and ends—with a synthesis of prior work.

Beyond that standard procedure, a stand-alone literature review usually covers a more extensive body of existing research without presenting new study findings. This can range from a compact essay that summarizes key findings in an area, to an all-encompassing, book-length mono-

23

graph that introduces new concepts and directions for future research. Occasionally, a diligent scholar's thorough review of a large body of related work almost becomes a career. Although each original study enhances our understanding of communication to some extent, a well-crafted literature review is more likely to move forward a body of knowledge as a whole. Synthesizing books and essays generally enjoy a long shelf life as reference works and textbooks, and creative literature reviews that construct new knowledge provide the field's landmark citations on many topics.

Despite the importance of synthesis to the advancement of knowledge, relatively few scholars in communication research undertake this kind of task. One reason for this dearth is that most graduate programs train students to conduct research projects, but teach little about writing more broadly about research. That is the subject of this chapter.

❖ PLANNING

Just as doing a study requires careful planning in the form of hypotheses and data collection, one does not simply sit down and begin writing a literature review. Explication of concepts (Chaffee, 1991) is just as essential a first step in preparing for a synthesis as it is in designing a study. Even when you know which studies you might want to include, it helps to give forethought to the ideas they represent so that you can organize your search for additional, related studies, sorting out those that belong from those that do not.

Organizing Concepts

A research literature is not an undifferentiated mass of discrete studies, and a literature review is not a mere stringing together of abstracts of studies that share some common theme. The first step toward a creative synthesis is to adopt an organizing scheme that can embrace a wide range of information. Although almost any classification system is preferable to none, some are better than others.

Many literature reviews classify studies into groups that share self-evident features and perhaps patterns of results. Research on use of household media, for example, might be sorted into studies of print, broadcast, and interactive media, or into studies of children, adolescents, and adults. The preferable category system is the one that lays bare important divisions in findings across studies. Categorizing studies by media, for example, enables you to see whether interactive media are functionally more similar to print or to broadcast channels. Sorting out analyses by age would be a good idea if there were notable differences in findings between family generations or between children and adolescents —or if there were no differences, but popular lore holds that there are. As these examples suggest, even simple classification schemes bear upon hypotheses of a sort.

Typically, hypotheses about communication involve causation in some way, perhaps because we study human communication in the hope of improving it as well as understanding it. Causation involves us in such metatheoretical concepts as independent variable (cause), dependent variable (effect), mediating processes that link the two, and contingent conditions that might be required for this link to operate. Each of these is a potential organizing theme for a literature review. For example, one could organize a synthesis in terms of different communication content or channels (independent variables), of different outcomes (dependent variables), or of different contingent conditions. Which you choose should be guided by your intentions, the findings in the literature at hand, and the kind of reader to whom the review is addressed.

Meaning Analysis

Because a literature review focuses on a single substantive hypothesis or idea across a variety of studies, careful qualitative analysis of meanings is needed. All concepts discussed in the review need to be defined at least preliminarily before one can begin searching out studies and deciding if they belong in the synthesis. Thus, the first step in explication, or meaning analysis, must to some extent precede collection of material from which the review will be fashioned. Often, this meaning analysis is rather casual and unstated, but there is one inherent value in setting it down formally: It can be featured in the introductory section of the literature review.

A meaning analysis requires some preliminary familiarity with at least part of the literature in question. Looking up a word's meanings in an unabridged dictionary can also be a useful first step. With a central term or phrase in hand, and with synonyms from the dictionary, relevant studies can be located via a *keyword search* of a bibliographic database.

Most literature reviewers today very soon turn to that procedure, letting the computer locate a corpus of information to be organized. However, first-stage keyword searches also tend to turn up a lot of material irrelevant to one's topic (because the same word means different things in different scholarly contexts) and to miss a great many relevant items (because scholars in different social sciences express the same idea in different terms). A computerized search for studies relating to "limited effects" of mass communication would, for example, miss political science studies related to "minimal consequences," which is simply another name for the same theory.

Even given such uncertainties, a preliminary pass through the literature enables the scholar to begin to sift through different meanings, and preliminarily order them in a way that could be useful for telling the story when it is fully compiled. This phase might be called "bringing order out of chaos." Although it does not usually involve writing in the usual, finished sense, as this phase proceeds the author is already thinking about possible ways to write the eventual synthesis.

One form of ordering is sometimes called a "tree of definitions." The concept "mass media," for example, has several branches, including electronic and print media. Growing out of each of these are narrower limbs such as periodicals (e.g., magazines and newspapers) and books from the print media branch, broadcast and video from the electronic branch, and so forth. Before long, the scholar is likely to notice two or three very common categories whose internal meaning structure needs to be further sorted out to address the issues covered in the literature review. Broadcast media, for example, can be divided into radio and television, or broadcast and cable, or public and commercial branches.

Empirical Analysis

Finding studies to incorporate into a literature review is the first step; picking out the ones to use is the next one, and it requires some rules. That is, having replaced mere names with meanings in the early stage of explication, you next need to replace abstract meanings with a clear sense of what kinds of evidence match them and how these concepts play out in actual research.

The principles of inclusion and exclusion constitute the beginning of empirical analysis, or definition in terms of researchable evidence. The shift from meaning analysis to empirical analysis is never complete, and

should not be. Abstract concepts must have understandable verbal refer-
ents so that we can communicate our theoretical ideas to other scholars,
which is after all the main purpose of a synthesizing literature review. But
a word or phrase, which evokes thoughts that go beyond what the author
intends, is never in itself as precise a way of conveying meaning as is a
concise definition of the concept it represents. For example, the word *media* includes artistic means, such as oil and watercolor painting; rarely,
however, would a communication scholar intend this referent. Even the
use of *media* to denote channels of communication is ambiguous; it is
commonly used to refer to both the technical means of message transmission and the institutions in which popular entertainment and news are
produced. At the beginning of a literature review, then, it is important to
provide at least a working definition of the concept in question. As research accumulates, this definition is given empirical meaning partly by
specifying what is excluded.

A great deal of thought should be put into defining boundaries, such
as where to draw the line between public and private communication. In
law, if defaming someone in a newspaper is libel but the same statement
in a letter to one person is not, how many people must receive the message before the line between the two is crossed? Research synthesis rarely
comes down to such a finely graded numerical level, but where should
we divide, say, interpersonal and mass communication, or one-way and
interactive communication? Are a metropolitan daily and a weekly
neighborhood shopper in the same city both simply "newspapers"? If
not, what marks the essential difference between them? Other scholars
can only know what you mean when you make it explicit, even if you are
using multiple criteria, such as circulation, staff size, news hole, wire ser-
vices, and the like.

These are not just questions about research; they affect teaching as
well. Different types of communication, such as interpersonal versus organizational versus mediated communication, are often covered in different courses, and even in separate departments in large universities. If
courses, like literature reviews, are to be coherent for their audiences,
then boundaries between them should be developed in the context of
real-world differences, such as the opportunity for feedback, control, and
tailoring of messages. Rules of inclusion and exclusion represent little
theories, and they are tested every time an author has to decide where to
put a new communication phenomenon, such as the Internet, or a new
variable, such as interactivity.

Even when one's concept is grounded in an empirical literature, such as those of diffusion, political communication, or human-computer interaction, the standard criteria for theory development are immediately applicable. This means, among other things, that one's working concepts, or preliminary terminology, should embrace most of what is known about the subject, and they should offer a means of resolving empirical irregularities or "anomalies" (Kuhn, 1970) by reorganizing assumptions, propositions, or research goals. One's organizing concepts should be provocative, pointing to additional research that needs to be done. This is one of the main goals of a literature review.

Operational Contingencies

Reviewing research across studies can identify between-studies variables that are, within any single study, constants and not variables. The year in which a study was conducted is a good example of such operational contingencies, because communication institutions change over time. Inferences that were drawn about the "newspaper" in the 1940s may not mean the same thing at all half a century later, when many newspapers have died in the face of competition from new media, when the surviving papers serve sprawling metropolitan regions instead of compact local communities, when most papers have moved to the political center editorially, when most are run by conglomerate corporations instead of autocratic family publishers, and when a sizeable portion of informed citizens get their news by other means. Television is different in degree perhaps, but not in kind; the three-network U.S. broadcasting scene of the 1960s is approximately as different from today's 70+ channel cable systems as are the European state-broadcasting systems of the 1960s from the competitive commercial systems in the same countries today.

Many other operational contingencies besides sheer historical setting should be examined in a productive literature review. Studies of communication involve people, and researchers tend to study people who are easily incorporated into their studies. A common complaint about laboratory experiments on communication, for example, is that they involve mainly college sophomores. This criticism is often lodged mindlessly, as if one would always get different results with older or less-educated subjects. Whether there is reason to expect contradictory findings with other populations should remain a matter of judgment. Better yet, it can become an issue for study. If a literature review finds that studies of people of varying ages or cultural backgrounds produce contrasting results, this can be the basis for further theorizing. What unexamined variables or operational contingencies might account for the difference?

For example, Martin, McNelly, and Izcaray (1976) were able to predict differences in adoption of mass media in Venezuela between urban residents who had recently migrated from the countryside and those who had lived in a city for a long time. The recent urban arrivals still exhibited the restricted patterns of media use that the literature review had indicated were common only in rural populations.

Methods of study are also operational contingencies. For instance, survey questions about the frequency of viewing television news, or the hours per day spent doing so, do not correlate appreciably with public affairs knowledge. However, when the question asks about "attention paid" to the news when it is on, or whether the person "tries to watch" the news, these indicators of more active seeking via television constitute as strong a predictor of public information as is newspaper reading (Chaffee & Schleuder, 1986). Discovery of this pattern not only improved the academic reputation of television news, it also affected the way survey scholars measure the independent variable of TV news consumption in relation to citizen competence.

Constructing the Empirical Definition

An empirical definition of a concept usually follows a considerable period of study, and is integral to a synthesis of a substantial body of research. Once many ideas have been tried out in the field so that we can see which ones have made a difference and which have turned out to be blind alleys, we are ready to make some conceptual decisions. Besides identifying boundaries, which tell what is excluded, explication of a concept requires that we specify its essential characteristics, or what is included. This is never an easy or finished matter.

Essential characteristics emerge from the interplay between a tentative definition and a large body of empirical findings. For example, in early sociology a fairly general definition of a *social system* distinguished between the functions of task performance and system maintenance (Merton, 1949). These two functions are presumed to be independent of one another and to apply to all social systems. Note that this dualistic conceptualization, which tells us two kinds of things a social system does, can exist without anyone ever "seeing" a social system. Indeed, the existence of a social system is more likely to be inferred from observing these two essential characteristics in operation than in literally observing it as an entity. The conception is, in effect, more important than the physical reality. When we notice people achieving something together (task performance) and also performing rituals that keep them together (system maintenance), we are likely to conclude that they constitute a social system. This kind of definition is, in essence, a hypothesis: If the people in question were to do nothing as a body, or failed to maintain their social cohesion, we should begin to doubt the supposition of a social system. Demographic categories that are given popular names (e.g., "Baby Boomers," "dead white males") do not necessarily function as social systems.

Boundary conditions are needed at the beginning of an empirical analysis, but they can also become problematic the more a concept is explored, and so we need to continually reestablish them as the study progresses. Communication research started in the United States and a few parallel European countries, but today it is spreading around the globe —where it encounters a lot of cross-cultural variation. Sometimes, a cross-cultural research team has trouble finding words to ask questions about some concepts, such as the Confucian tradition of filial piety in the United States, or the American recognition of a right to privacy in China (Pan, Chaffee, Chu, & Ju, 1994).

❖ SYNTHESIZING

There are no rules for the crucial activity of synthesizing a collection of studies, but it is analogous to telling a story. That is, there needs to be a narrative progression within the overall exposition. Like any story, it needs a beginning, a middle, and an end. Compared with most stories, however, the typical literature review contains a long middle between a concise introduction and an even briefer ending. This large middle includes several major sections, but only rarely will they fall into a chronological sequence the way the parts of a story line do. The author has to devise a sequence that suits the content and to decide which themes to highlight. If one section will review a great deal of research relative to the others, most authors present that topic first. That way the reader gets the main thrust of the literature early on, and the author then covers topics that researchers have been neglecting.

An Ongoing Process

A literature review never literally ends, although for purposes of writing, of course, it must come to a close for the time being. Theorizing, which is the central activity in synthesizing research, can be pictured as a kind of dialogue between theory and data, between abstract terms and operational definitions, between timeless generalizations and their real-world manifestations in particular times and settings. This is another way of stating that theorizing is an ongoing process. Only a now-sterile theory could be presented as a finished product, with no further research or reinterpretation needed. When a scholar presents a synthesis of communication research and pronounces it "finished," it is probably better described as a product of ideology than of open investigation.

Organizing the Synthesis

There are many ways to organize a synthesis of the literature, but the choice you make is probably the major factor determining whether the final product is a success or failure. So we will consider a number of approaches that have led to success for some scholars. First, we discuss the advantages of organizing according to independent variable and dependent variable categories, which are two of the most common designs. We then present examples of five other successful approaches to the organization of a literature review.

Independent Variable Categories. When a communication technology or industry is new and its effects not yet well understood, literature reviews are often organized by independent variables, such as media. For example, as newspaper chains and joint operating agreements proliferated in the 1970s, many studies compared the news content produced by these new economic structures to that of the older structures of family-owned local papers. The same thing was done in the 1950s with television, a new medium whose audiences were compared to those of radio, newspapers, movies, and magazines. Later, the audiences and content of cable TV were compared to those of conventional broadcast channels. In the

1980s, such innovations as videocassettes, satellite broadcasting, and computer-based communication were lumped together as "new communication technologies," a label that betrayed the absence of any conceptual definition; these media had only recently been introduced into people's lives. As categories are refined, they can be differentiated in terms of their functions rather than simply their names. This is an important step in explication, the intellectual transition from mere nominal definition to real definition in the form of meaning analysis.

Organization of media by their social functions, or meanings, is useful to practitioners who are trying to devise the optimal means of achieving a desired outcome. This viewpoint was epitomized by Wilbur Schramm's (1977) general advice to strategists in developing countries, embodied in his book title, *Big Media, Little Media*. Originally an advocate of "modernization" of agricultural economies using mass communication, Schramm had learned after years of field evaluations that more modest "little media" tailored to local populations can accomplish more in the real world.

Dependent Variable Categories. As a body of research moves forward, the field needs syntheses that focus on outcomes, or dependent variables. This approach can show researchers which outcomes have been tested and which ones have been found. Communication practitioners can use this information to achieve specific results, such as learning or behavior change. The dependent variable approach is exemplified by the work of Albert Bandura (1997), whose social cognitive theory has been widely used in applied behavioral science. Reviewing the literature on self-efficacy and health behavior change, Bandura analyzed research findings on the ways various health education interventions led to desired results. The subheadings in the review were all conceived in terms of outcomes: "achievement of personal change," "maintenance of personal change," "relapse prevention and management," "self-management of chronic diseases," "social diffusion of health-promoting practices," and so on. Practitioners hoping to achieve one or another of the behavioral changes could draw on Bandura's review for guidelines.

A literature review focusing on children and the then-new technologies of interactive media (Lieberman, 1985) was organized into five types of outcomes that had been examined in research up to that time: (a) children's *usage* of interactive media, including influences on computer and video game access, ownership, and use; and effects of interactive media on young people's (b) *learning,* (c) *cognitive skills,* (d) *attitudes* about the technology and its users, and (e) *social relationships.* This overview of a newly developing research area identified the types of outcomes that had been tested, and in so doing could also point to potential outcomes that researchers had not yet addressed.

It should be clear that one could synthesize the same body of research according to either an independent or dependent variable organization. The choice should be made consciously, with an eye to one's main purpose. For example, the literature on political campaign effects could be organized around administrative advice about how to build a candidate's name recognition, attract donations, improve perceived electability, and gain votes (dependent variable organization). Or it could be organized around possible reforms of campaign communication policy, such as limitations on fund raising, length of the campaign, and advertising ploys (independent variable organization). Yet another approach might be to evaluate how democratic ideals are served, for good or ill, by such standard practices as party conventions, televised debates, horse race coverage, and election day vote projections (independent variable organization). Research on such variables as party identification, political knowledge, and time of voting decision would be relevant to each of these literature reviews, but would be organized quite differently depending on whether they were examined in the context of independent or dependent variables.

In the next five sections, we point out several different bases for organizing a body of communication research, using some excellent examples of the genre. We discuss five approaches: organization according to (a) a structural model of the communication phenomenon, (b) a process model of the phenomenon, (c) traditions of research based on alternative empirical assumptions about how best to study the phenomenon, (d) traditions based on contrasting normative views of the phenomenon, and (e) the device of relating one research literature to another. Although these are by no means the only possibilities, discussing them should give the reader (and potential writer) ideas about how to proceed.

A Structural Model: Mass Communication. One form of synthesis is to assert a general model of the structure of a communication phenomenon and then sort studies to fit under each category. An example that was very useful in getting communication started as a field of study (although it later became quite controversial) is Lasswell's (1948) suggestion that an act of communication may be described as the answer to five questions: (a) Who (b) says what (c) in which channel (d) to whom (e) with what effect? Among the objections to this model are that it is unidirectional (i.e., not two-way or interactive), and that it assumes that the ultimate question is a task-oriented effect, rather than, say, simply holding a society together via shared ritual communication.

The five queries, however, were put to use immediately, as the first few dozen studies of mass communication began appearing in print. Hovland (1954) and Schramm (1962), for example, both used this scheme to sort out the research on mass communication for the field of psychology. Lasswell's five questions represented, respectively, control analysis, content analysis, audience analysis, channel analysis, and effects analysis. A structural organization of the literature is useful for summarizing what scholars think is known, and how different bodies of work relate to one another.

A Process Model: Diffusion. It is sometimes possible to lay out a theory in sequential terms and divide it according to distinct phases of a common process. This approach is exemplified by *Diffusion of Innovations* by Everett Rogers (1962), a dissertation literature review that became a classic text of communication research. The key phenomenon in diffusion analysis is the cumulative S-curve, which tracks the acceptance of an innovation by members of a social system over time. Rogers distinguished several stages in the process, such as initial awareness of an innovation and its eventual use, each of which has its own S-curve over time. Examining hundreds of case studies in his synthesis, he found that initial awareness often comes from mass media, but adoption is associated more with interpersonal discussion. This knowledge has in turn been quite useful around the world in planning the introduction of subsequent new ideas and practices.

Rogers was prescient in his selection of *an innovation* as the core concept by which all else in a diffusion process is defined. Once the unit of an innovation was fixed upon, studies of very different innovations could be analyzed within a common framework, enabling him to formulate many generalizations about the role of communication in social change.

Alternative Empirical Assumptions: Interpersonal Communication. Another technique is to compare and contrast the assumptions that are made within different traditions of research. This enables the reader to grasp not only the research, but also the beliefs that lie behind it, and to choose a career path that is consistent with a personal preference for a way of thinking. For example, Gerald Miller (1978) summed up decades of research on interpersonal communication in a review article comparing the theoretical assumptions guiding each of four kinds of study: (a) the situational approach, (b) the developmental approach, (c) the law-governed approach, and (d) the rule-governed approach. He then pointed out how each of these generates a different kind of knowledge about communication.

The situational approach examines how interpersonal communication differs from one situation to the next. This involves such variables as the number of communicators, the physical distance separating them, the number of sensory channels they can use, and the immediacy of feedback from one person to another. Interpersonal communication is differentiated from mass communication by being low on the first two of these criteria and high on the last two. The developmental approach assumes in effect that all communicative transactions begin at zero, which is to say they are impersonal at first. The problem studied is how, over time, communication between two people becomes more interpersonal and what factors foster this process. The laws approach is that of conventional social science, in which it is assumed that communication behavior is subject to certain lawful regularities. The purpose of research is to find out what these laws are by empirically testing hypotheses. The rules approach, by contrast, makes no such general assumptions. It simply holds that a set of people will communicate according to a set of internally defined rules by which they control their actions toward one another. Research, instead of being a "search for laws," becomes a more modest inquiry into the rules that are being followed by specific people in specific times and places.

Miller's synthesis was designed to help other scholars locate their own research in a more general scheme. This kind of theory-based analysis is rarely possible until many kinds of studies have accumulated in the literature of a field.

Contrasting Normative Views: Pornography. Not all theories of communication are motivated simply by scientific curiosity; in mass communication especially, there is a strong normative component as well. That is, theories are as much about how communication *ought to be* as they are about how it is.

Normative theories generally grow out of an ideological position in which the assumptions are morally grounded. Because not everyone shares a common ideological view of everything people do, there are contrasting normative approaches to many communication phenomena that can be used in organizing a literature. This kind of analysis makes clear why some forms of research are done and why not everyone considers them of equal pertinence.

The subject of pornography, always a hotbed of moral dispute, was analyzed in terms of three normative approaches by Daniel Linz and Neil Malamuth (1993). Before outlining their own approach, the relatively new (a) feminist tradition, they contrasted the predominant (b) conservative-moralist and (c) liberal schools of thought and public policy. They not only compared these three traditions in terms of empirical assumptions, terminology, characteristic study designs, salient findings, and legal implications, but also traced their grounding in differing normative assumptions.

Within the conservative-moralist tradition, erotic media portrayals are characterized as "obscenity" and are deemed to be patently offensive. This means that possible effects are to an extent beside the point: The main research activity is pejorative content analysis. Some effects studies, though, explore the impact of pornography and therefore address conservative-moralist concerns, such as family values (Zillmann & Bryant, 1988), or general arousal of antisocial behaviors, such as aggression between males (Zillmann, Bryant, & Carveth, 1981).

In the liberal tradition, by sharp contrast, what a moralist would call obscenity is characterized more neutrally as "erotica" and viewed as essentially harmless. Consequently, research tends to consist of audience analysis, probing why people consume sexually oriented media materials. Most of the reasons given are positive ones; adult consumers tend to enjoy erotica (Presidential Commission on Obscenity and Pornography, 1970), and the approach to policy within this tradition is largely permissive.

Finally, the feminist tradition zeroes in on the danger that violent pornography poses to women. Experiments concentrate on such effects as audience members' desensitization to rape and on policy recommendations geared toward establishing a community climate that condemns the dissemination of violent pornography.

By following through from normative approaches to empirical research to policy, Linz and Malamuth (1993) provide a useful overview for classroom teaching. Students with differing values can nonetheless appreciate alternative points of view and understand the total body of research better than if taught within only one of the three traditions.

Relating Two Types of Research: Television Violence. A synthesis can be especially helpful in shaping research of one type based on findings from another type of research on the same subject. The national television violence study of 1995–1998, an ambitious content analysis headed by Barbara Wilson (Wilson, Kunkel, Linz, & Potter, 1997), began not just with a review of prior content analyses, but with a more basic synthesis of controlled experiments on media violence and aggression. Then in the content analysis, current TV programs were classified according to features that have been shown in laboratory work either to strengthen or to diminish subjects' tendencies to behave aggressively toward other people.

This content analysis enriched the effects literature by showing that most violence on American television is presented in ways that render viewer aggression more likely. For instance, TV violence, particularly on cable channels, is usually justified within the story line and viewers are rarely shown any negative consequences for the victims. The literature review explicitly connected the two bodies of research—that is, from experiments and from content analyses—so that they became mutually reinforcing in terms of their implications for families and for public policy.

Caution: Do Not Overgeneralize

We have stressed here that a literature review can have a powerful influence on both future research and practice within a field of communication. This places extra responsibility on the author. Understanding that one's synthesis will guide how others think and act, one should exercise care in making empirical claims. The impulse to overclaim is a natural one in academics, where generality of theory is prized. However, it can backfire on a field that is led down the wrong path by a parsimonious and persuasive, but somewhat irresponsible, tale.

Limited Effects: A Too-Powerful Synthesis. An example of a synthesis that had enormous influence on communication study and practice is the model of limited effects of mass communication. It illustrates both the power of a broad synthesis and the potential problems that can arise when more breadth is claimed than is warranted by the evidence. It began modestly enough, but mushroomed in the 1940s and 1950s, an era when social scientists, new at their craft, tried to couch their conclusions as if they could be generalized to practically all people in all times and places. Eventually, the field came to see this model as limited in its applicability, but in its heyday its theoretical power was as great as the once-feared media power that it portrayed as highly restricted.

Limited effects began with a few interviewer notes from a survey of voters in the presidential election campaign of 1940 (Lazarsfeld, Berelson, & Gaudet, 1944). Although the researchers were looking for evidence of powerful campaign rhetoric that might swing the election to one major party or the other, some respondents volunteered that they had been influenced instead by other people they knew. This observation was expanded into two related concepts, the "two-step flow of communication" and "opinion leaders" (Berelson, Lazarsfeld, & McPhee, 1954). Opinion leaders were essentially peers who intervened between the mass media and everyone else; they were pictured as an intermediate step in a two-step flow of influence that often counteracted propaganda, and even news, from the mass media. Other people were defined as the main source of influence in public opinion processes, as they were in the adoption of innovations (Katz, 1957; Katz & Lazarsfeld, 1955).

Joseph T. Klapper (1949, 1960) synthesized the limited effects model in one of the most far-reaching literature reviews in the history of communication—it was even accepted as a dissertation in lieu of an original empirical study (Klapper, 1961)—featuring the two-step flow from media through opinion leaders. Klapper and other Lazarsfeld proteges (e.g., Berelson & Steiner, 1964) established limited effects as the dominant interpretation of mass communication as a whole, and it discouraged study of political mass communication for several decades (Chaffee & Hochheimer, 1983). Eventually its influence on thought and scholarship receded, in the face of evidence of predominantly direct effects of media news (e.g., Chaffee, Ward, & Tipton, 1970; Deutschmann & Danielson, 1960; McCombs & Shaw, 1972). Interpersonal communication, however, continued to show up as an important factor in adoption of such innovations as new communication technologies, and today interpersonal influence occupies a central role in that literature (Rogers, 1983). There is no rule for defining the range of applicability of a general, though not universal, principle in synthesizing communication research. One must continue to process new findings, note anomalies, and consider circumscribing each knowledge claim.

Strength of Findings. An important responsibility in writing a literature review is to assess the strength of a relationship. Social research methodology, although often portrayed as quantitative in nature, is only superficially so when it comes to reporting the conclusions that become the raw data for a literature review. The general method of communication research is to derive hypotheses from a theory, and to test each hypothesis in a kind of true-false fashion. That is, each research proposition is tested against the null hypothesis, and if it is statistically significant— that is, nonzero—it is simply accepted in the form of a qualitative statement. This tells us whether there is any relationship, but not how important it is relative to other factors. Readers of a synthesis deserve that additional kind of judgment based on the overall record.

Quantitative strength of relationships is difficult to assess given the field's chronic measurement error, nonnormal distributions, and incomplete operationalizations of most communication concepts. Although there have been some advances in statistical procedures for meta-analysis of an empirical literature on a single oft-studied hypothesis, such as the impact of media violence on aggressive behavior (Paik & Comstock, 1994), the author of a synthesis usually faces a welter of knowledge claims that must first be dealt with qualitatively, and then in some quantitative perspective. As a result, quantitative interpretations in syntheses tend to be based on the summary percentage of studies that end with a particular qualitative conclusion, rather than on the strength of the findings within those studies. This can be misleading in the case of a consistent but weak relationship. For instance, an enthusiastic literature review might state that "more than 90% of all studies show a positive correlation" even when the correlations in question never exceed $r = 0.20$.

Note the Research Setting. Another difficulty facing the synthesizer of research is generalizing findings from each particular research setting to the larger context to which one might apply them. The setting includes the time and place of a study, such as the historical and political situation surrounding an election campaign or the media resources and voting history of the community in which a study of media power is conducted. Authors, both of original research and of syntheses, are justified in speculating that a new finding *might* apply quite widely, but that means further research is in order.

The working assumption of all empirical study—that each hypothesis is open to further testing—can easily be forgotten in the rush of drawing conclusions. For instance, the Lazarsfeld group's (Lazarsfeld,

Berelson, & Gaudet, 1944) studies were all conducted in midsized communities of the northeastern United States, minor industrial hubs surrounded by farmlands. The authors' emphasis on interpersonal influence would not necessarily apply even to New York City. They considered that metropolis atypical; but so, perhaps, were the small cities they studied (Chaffee & Hochheimer, 1983). Diffusion of innovations is, as a rule, also studied in close-knit communities, for example in agrarian settings and among elite urban professionals (Coleman, Menzel, & Katz, 1958). When Klapper (1960) came to write his synthesis showing limited media effects, though, these contextual details were stripped away. Perhaps even more serious in terms of overgeneralization, findings from the era of radio were applied theoretically—with little or no empirical testing—to the new era of television.

❖ WRITING

Readers expect a literature review to help them learn a lot without their having to work too hard. To this end, an author's language should be accessible to a wide range of people. The most successful syntheses, such as those we have described above, were crafted so that students new to the subject could read them without a lot of prior preparation. The general rules of writing for the public, such as choosing the shorter or more common word where possible and writing straightforward declarative sentences, are more necessary in a literature review than in more technical forms of research writing.

This does not mean avoiding specialized terminology: It means teaching it. Often, this can be done by an appositive paraphrase, a capsule definition (such as this one) that immediately follows an unusual term. This is especially important in describing communication research, which is full of everyday terms that have more specialized meanings within the academic field. For example, most people do not distinguish between *opinions* and *beliefs,* but in describing a study that does a writer should explain the difference that is meant.

Novel Terminology and Labels

A synthesizer must be alert to new concepts that have been created within the literature being reviewed. Novel terms and phrases that introduce truly new ideas should be explained fully, even if the original author only defined by example. Not every neologism that someone dreams up is worth preserving, of course; you must exercise judgment in selecting those you think might have a long future in the field.

An example of the power of new terminology is the concept of *agenda setting,* a phrase coined by Maxwell McCombs and Donald Shaw (1972) when they found that the political issues voters considered most important were those that had been given the most coverage in the press. Although other scholars had noted this tendency before, no felicitous term had previously captured it and only it. Lazarsfeld and Merton (1960) had, for instance, called it "status conferral on an issue," an idea that was overshadowed by their companion hypothesis that media coverage is a source of "status conferral on a person." Once the term *agenda setting* entered the literature, though, it caught on rapidly; it has been the topic of numerous literature reviews and more than 100 original studies (Dearing & Rogers, 1996).

Reaching a Wide Range of Readers

A common mistake in writing mass communication research is to assume that the reader is familiar with American television or with the news of a particular era, such as Watergate, and will readily recognize examples of names that are indelibly imprinted in the mind of the writer. The essence of preparing ideas for a more general readership is to make them understandable for people who will read them in other times and places. Communication literature from the present-day United States, synthesized from studies done in previous decades, needs to be communicated to students of the future and in many countries.

Two popular writing devices fall short of these goals: mere quotation of a term and inserting the word *like* without further explanation. To put quotation marks around the phrase "pseudo-opinions," for instance, is no substitute for defining it; somewhere the author needs to explain that this term refers to answers that people give in public surveys when in fact they had no opinion before the interview. Similarly, the phrase "programs like *All in the Family*" will probably fail to inform a reader in Korea in 2002 what kind of program the author has in mind. An accompanying description, such as "spicy" or "politically controversial," or a substitute noun, such as "situation comedy," can help the reader get oriented to a foreign or dated example.

These are only common examples of a frequent failing in literature reviews. In editing, it is useful to go through your esoteric terms and examples, and ask yourself if they will be understandable to future students who do not share your particular life history, particularly those who live in other cultures. Doing this will not only make your synthesis more readable, it will force you to explain conceptually ideas that are in your head but not necessarily in the head of every reader.

Focus on Research Conclusions

The point of most literature reviews is to convey what is known, not how it came to be known. When writing up research, one normally tells what the questions were, how the data were gathered, and then what the results and conclusions were. When synthesizing this into a literature review, however, it is the conclusions that should be highlighted, with just enough supporting information to make clear what the questions were and the nature of the data. Only if you consider a conclusion to be suspect because of deficiencies in the study is it useful to describe research methods. Here is a fictitious but typical example of a passage from a literature review as originally written and then as rewritten by an editor:

> Before: "In a 1981 study, Twickenham observed communication between doctors and nurses through a one-way window in a New Mexico hospital. She coded utterances as either giving or asking, and either opinion or information. She reported that doctors tended to ask for information and to give opinions, while nurses instead tended to give information. These differences were statistically significant at the $p < 0.001$ level."
>
> After: "In doctor-nurse interaction, doctors tend to ask for information and to give opinions, while nurses mainly give information (Twickenham, 1981)."

Note that in this example only the inferences are described, not the details of how those inferences were reached. That is probably all that is needed; most readers are unlikely to be interested in evaluating the study itself. Someone who wants to do that can readily check out the original research from the citation.

Note also that the inferences are stated in present tense, as the reason for your reporting this finding is that you think the generalization holds for other times and places. Its truth value would be enhanced, of course, if several other citations could be added (i.e., similar studies that found approximately the same thing). Readers are looking for general principles, and much of the writing of a literature review involves searching across studies for statements that seem to be consistently supported. Your review should point out this consistency of result, leaving the vagaries of research methods to each individual published study.

Intended Audiences

A writer must think of the literature review from the perspective of the reader. This begins with forming a fairly clear idea of the likely audience. It is generally advisable to assume a broad readership that includes nonspecialists, such as students in an advanced or even introductory college course. Professors often assign syntheses rather than single studies, because emphasis on technical details can get in the way of communicating the ideas that are at stake in the research.

Still, the primary addressees for most syntheses of research are other researchers, and for them the product should be presented in the form of theory. Findings should be organized and described to help researchers understand the studies' contributions to what you hope will become an upward spiral of theory, hypothesis, test, finding, revised theory, further tests, and so on. Literature reviews can also be intended for use by communication practitioners, such as those designing messages, interfaces, publications, and the like, and those in communicatory roles, such as teachers, parents, and managers. In between these two potential audiences, researchers and practitioners, there are a number of academics who might consult a literature review to gather a general understanding of a research topic although they do not intend to conduct research on it themselves. Instructors are also often grateful to find a literature review that they can turn into a class lecture. Because these latter two audiences, the practitioners and the academic nonspecialists (and their students), do not share the detailed background of scientists who are active in a research area, it is best to couch one's essay in terms that will be widely understandable among educated and interested readers. In short, a literature review should be designed as a teaching tool.

Although it is not always possible, a writer should try to aim a literature review at all three kinds of readers. This means drawing conclusions not only about (a) what has been found to date (for the academic nonspecialist) and (b) what should be studied next in order to advance theory (for the avid researcher), but also about (c) what these findings mean for the practice of communication and how they might be applied in specific instances (for the practitioner). These kinds of conclusions correspond roughly to the initial (a) research summary section, and the concluding (b) implications and (c) applications sections, which surround the operational details that comprise the middle of an original research article or thesis.

When geared to communication practitioners, a literature review can turn research conclusions into practical advice about content, formats, instructional techniques, or communication settings that are effective for specific types of people. Lieberman and Linn (1991) used this approach in a literature review about computers and the development of self-directed learning skills. Applying findings from the research literature, they concluded the review with ten recommendations for designing software and computer-based activities to support and improve self-directed learning. Rice and Atkin (1994) presented principles of communication campaign design that grew out of a combination of research evidence and successful practice in the field. Each step they recommended in the campaign design process was justified with research evidence that substantiated the appropriateness of their conclusions; they also noted counterevidence when the literature contained conflicting findings. This approach allows each reader to weigh the authors' conclusions against competing points of view, and to adapt the collected knowledge to specific field problems.

❖ CONCLUSION

A synthesizing literature review can introduce new research concepts, explicate existing concepts more clearly, advance theory, provide an overview of the current state of research in a field, and guide communication practitioners. It can discuss the implications of past findings and point to directions for further research and application. Furthermore, by aggregating findings across time, place, media, messages, or audience types, it can identify evidence of broader trends than any single study might yield.

Literature reviews are invaluable references for scholars, interested academics, and practitioners alike; many of the communication field's groundbreaking works are literature reviews. It would behoove all communication scholars to pay close attention to the literature reviews they write in the opening paragraphs of their research articles, and to publish longer essays or books synthesizing the literature in their research areas. The field of communication, as a young and growing discipline, offers great rewards for the scholar who puts in the effort to codify knowledge in this indispensable form.

❖ REFERENCES

Bandura, A. (1997). *Self-efficacy: The exercise of control.* New York: Freeman.

Berelson, B., Lazarsfeld, P., & McPhee, W. (1954). *Voting: A study of opinion formation in a presidential campaign.* Chicago: University of Chicago Press.

Berelson, B., & Steiner, G. (1964). *Human behavior: An inventory of scientific findings.* New York: Harcourt, Brace & World.

Chaffee, S. (1991). *Communication concepts 1: Explication.* Newbury Park, CA: Sage.

Chaffee, S., & Hochheimer, J. (1983). Mass communication in national election campaigns: The research experience in the United States. In W. Schulz & K. Schonbach (Eds.), *Mass media and elections: International research perspectives* (pp. 65–103). Munich: Verlag.

Chaffee, S., & Schleuder, J. (1986). Measurement and effects of attention to media news. *Human Communication Research, 13,* 76–107.

Chaffee, S., Ward, S., & Tipton, L. (1970). Mass communication and political socialization. *Journalism Quarterly, 47,* 647–659, 666.

Coleman, J., Menzel, H., & Katz, E. (1958). Social processes in physicians' adoption of a new drug. *Journal of Chronic Diseases, 8,* 1–19.

Dearing, J., & Rogers, E. (1996). *Communication concepts 6: Agenda-setting.* Newbury Park, CA: Sage.

Deutschmann, P., & Danielson, W. (1960). Diffusion of the major news story. *Journalism Quarterly, 37,* 345–355.

Hovland, C. (1954). Effects of the mass media of communication. In G. Lindzey (Ed.), *Handbook of social psychology, Vol. 2: Special fields and applications* (pp. 1062–1103). Cambridge, MA: Addison-Wesley.

Katz, E. (1957). The two-step flow of communication: An up-to-date report on an hypothesis. *Public Opinion Quarterly, 21,* 61–78.

Katz, E., & Lazarsfeld, P. (1955). *Personal influence: The part played by people in the flow of mass communications.* Glencoe, IL: Free Press.

Klapper, J. T. (1949). *The effects of mass media.* New York: Columbia University Bureau of Applied Social Research.

Klapper, J. T. (1960). *The effects of mass communication.* New York: Free Press.

Klapper, J. T. (1961). *The effects of mass communication: An analysis of research on the effectiveness and limitations of mass media in influencing the opinions, values, and behavior of their audiences.* Doctoral dissertation, Columbia University, New York.

Kuhn, T. (1970). *The structure of scientific revolutions* (2nd ed.). Chicago: University of Chicago Press.

Lasswell, H. (1948). The structure and function of communication in society. In L. Bryson (Ed.), *The communication of ideas* (pp. 37–51). New York: Harper.

Lazarsfeld, P., Berelson, B., & Gaudet, H. (1944). *The people's choice: How the voter makes up his mind in a presidential campaign.* New York: Duell, Sloan & Pearce.

Lazarsfeld, P., & Merton, R. (1960). Mass communication, popular taste, and organized social action. In L. Bryson (Ed.), *The communication of ideas* (pp. 95–118). New York: Harper. (Original work published in 1948).

Lieberman, D. A. (1985). Research on children and microcomputers: A review of utilization and effects studies. In M. Chen & W. Paisley (Eds.), *Children and microcomputers: Research on the newest medium* (pp. 59–83). Beverly Hills, CA: Sage.

Lieberman, D. A., & Linn, M. C. (1991). Learning to learn revisited: Computers and the development of self-directed learning skills. *Journal of Research on Computing in Education, 23*(3), 373–395.

Linz, D., & Malamuth, N. (1993). *Communication concepts: Pornography.* Newbury Park, CA: Sage.

Martin, R., McNelly, J., & Izcaray, F. (1976). Is media use unidimensional? A socioeconomic approach. *Journalism Quarterly, 53,* 619–625.

McCombs, M., & Shaw, D. (1972). The agenda-setting function of mass media. *Public Opinion Quarterly, 36,* 176–187.

Merton, R. (1949). *Social theory and social structure.* New York: Free Press.

Miller, G. (1978). The current status of theory and research in interpersonal communication. *Human Communication Research, 4,* 164–178.

Paik, H., & Comstock, G. (1994). The effects of television violence on antisocial behavior: A meta-analysis. *Communication Research, 21,* 516–546.

Pan, Z., Chaffee, S., Chu, G., & Ju, Y. (1994). *To see ourselves: Comparing traditional Chinese and American cultural values.* Boulder, CO: Westview.

Presidential Commission on Obscenity and Pornography. (1970). *Technical reports of the Presidential Commission on Obscenity and Pornography.* Washington, DC: Government Printing Office.

Rice, R., & Atkin, C. (1994). Principles of successful public communication campaigns. In J. Bryant & D. Zillmann (Eds.), *Media effects: Advances in theory and research* (pp. 365–387). Hillsdale, NJ: Lawrence Erlbaum.

Rogers, E. (1962). *Diffusion of innovations.* New York: Free Press.

Rogers, E. (1983). *Diffusion of innovations* (3rd ed.). New York: Free Press.

Schramm, W. (1977). *Big media, little media: Tools and technologies for instruction.* Beverly Hills, CA: Sage.

Schramm, W. (1962). Mass communication. *Annual Review of Psychology, 13,* 251–284.

Wilson, B. J., Kunkel, D., Linz, D., & Potter, J. (1997). Violence in television programming overall. *National television violence study* (Vol. 1). Thousand Oaks, CA: Sage.

Zillmann, D., & Bryant, J. (1988). Effects of prolonged consumption of pornography on family values. *Journal of Family Issues, 9,* 518–544.

Zillmann, D., Bryant, J., & Carveth, R. A. (1981). The effect of erotica featuring sadomasochism and bestiality on motivated intermale aggression. *Personality and Social Psychology Bulletin, 7,* 153–159.

The Challenge of
Writing the Theoretical Essay

Judee K. Burgoon

❖ ❖ ❖

An oft-heard lament among communication scholars is that there are too few theories in our published literature. One possible reason for this is that scholars are frequently unsure as to what constitutes a theory. Can it be as succinct as Einstein's theory of relativity? Need it be as formal as a mathematical equation? Does a model or taxonomy qualify? How much "flesh" must a theoretical skeleton have before it is granted the status of a theory? The nebulousness of the criteria that must be met, coupled with wide variability across disciplines in what counts as theory, makes it unsurprising that many scholars are reluctant to label their work "a theory," opting instead for the more modest approach of proposing hypotheses, models, and the like.

However, if we heed Kaplan's (1964) claim that nothing is so practical as a good theory and realize that the primary objective is to purchase us greater insight into the world around us—greater ability to predict, explain, and/or control some phenomenon of interest—then we need not

47

be fainthearted about attempting to develop a theory. What follows are some practical guidelines for undertaking such an endeavor. These are by no means the only or necessarily a superior approach to theory construction; they simply represent a distillation of guidance that I have gleaned from my own mentors and colleagues, from scholarly writings on the process of theory development, and from my personal experiences in attempting to formulate several different theories of human interaction.

❖ REMEMBER THAT A THEORY
   IS IN A STATE OF "BECOMING"

Theories are dynamic, not static. They are evolving entities, not finished products. At the core of science is the concept of tentativeness. We advance theories in hopes of gaining greater understanding and heurism with them than without them. However, they are still speculative. They are open to being rejected or modified once subjected to public scrutiny and rigorous empirical testing or criticism. A commitment to developing and writing about theory obligates the writer to a stance of uncertainty. The point of theory development is incremental improvements in our knowledge base: what behavior modification folks call successive approximations, not final answers. Theories are never proven: They either gain support or they fail to gain support. The fact that they may be contested, discarded, and replaced can feel threatening, yet it also frees the writer to be wrong. Like a work of art, the process of shaping, modifying, and transforming a theory is itself a liberating activity, as long as one is not too ego invested in a particular point of view. Put differently, you have to love the process of inquiry, not the product itself, and to welcome the challenges and modifications that inevitably follow a theory's debut if you are going to make theory development a serious pursuit.

❖ STAKE OUT YOUR TERRITORY FOR THE READER

Sometimes authors begin a paper with an interesting quotation or anecdote or they chronicle some historical trends in the literature, but they neglect to tell readers exactly what their topic is. Readers need to get their bearings in order to be located somewhere in conceptual space and time. Early in the manuscript, then, the domain and scope of the theory need to be evident. Is the work about individual, dyadic, group, organizational, mediated, or public communication? Is it concerned with description, interpretation, antecedents to or consequences of communication, or social critique? Is it a macrolevel or microlevel examination of some phenomenon? Are you offering a bird's-eye or worm's-eye view, an insider's (i.e., emic) or an outsider's (i.e., etic) perspective? In short, how much terrain are you trying to cover, and from what vantage point will you do so?

As illustration, when I first began writing about nonverbal expectancy violations, I was only looking at personal space. I was interested in the social consequences of violating personal space for such outcomes as comprehension of what a violator said, attraction toward the violator, the impact on a violator's credibility, and willingness to comply with a violator's request. It was important that my co-authors and I make clear that our domain was nonverbal behavior but that our scope was fairly narrow. We were not talking about all manner of nonverbal violations, just ones related to proximity or distance. We were not talking about the causes of violations, only their effects. And, we were not talking about all manner of effects, just ones that had special relevance to communication. Later, when we expanded the theory to cover a wide range of nonverbal behaviors, we changed the theory's name accordingly. However, in the interest of simplicity and because a name can never describe all of a theory's content, it has been our obligation to inform readers whether we think the theory is applicable to verbal as well as nonverbal phenomena and to behavioral confirmations as well as violations.

This last point brings up a related caveat that should definitely count as one of the first principles of writing about communication theory: *Make sure it is about communication.* That statement may seem self-evident, but it is remarkable how often people who claim to be investigating communication actually have little interest in communication itself. Their interest may lie in some anthropological, sociological, psychological, or biological phenomenon in which communication *per se* plays an ancillary role. For example, decades of research have examined how individual difference variables (e.g., Machiavellianism, stimulus screening, gender, or cognitive heuristics) correlate with yet other individual difference variables (e.g., central v. peripheral information processing, attitudes toward health, attachment style). This is not to say these are not worthy topics, but if communication itself gets lost in the shuffle, then these really are not communication theories.

The fact that communication scholars so frequently find themselves wandering into others' "territory" feeds the claim that communication is a derivative discipline with no real theories of its own. I regard that as an unfair indictment. Our discipline by its very nature informs and is informed by many other disciplines, and so we are going to overlap with other fields of study. I have always been fond of a perspective attributed to the eminent psychologist Donald Campbell. He was said to embrace a "fish scale" model of disciplines, in which each, like the scales of a fish, overlapped with other related cognates in a very natural and functional manner. Whereas other fields may tend toward a "telescopic" (or what some might view as a parochial) approach to what is within their purview, communication, with its polyglot heritage, traditionally has taken a more panoramic (or what some might view as an eclectic) approach. Unlike the proverbial blind men who will only ever "know" their small part of the elephant's anatomy, communication scholars often strive to take in the "bigger picture." (I will say more about the downside risks of this later.) Thus, it is perfectly permissible to "borrow" theories or parts of theories from other fields, as long as you give proper credit when doing so and as long as you can articulate not only why what you have to offer is original but also how it differs from the other theories upon which you are drawing.

So, begin by clearly staking out the locus and boundaries of your topic. Then make sure that communication factors into it somehow.

❖ ANSWER THE QUESTION,
    "WHAT IS YOUR QUESTION?"

Far too often, enthusiastic students have come for approval to write about something that interests them, only to have me ask, "But what is your question?" It is not enough that your topic be "about" something —television violence, marital interaction patterns, coping with chronic illness, new technologies in the workplace. There must be some problem, issue, claim, or puzzling phenomenon that piqued your interest in the first place. That underlying question should be your starting place. In other words, *problematize* your topic: Put into words what intrigues you and what question or questions your theory is intended to answer. Then tell the reader what that question is. Nothing is more frustrating for reviewers than to find themselves 10 pages into a manuscript still waiting to find out what the proposed theory is supposed to cover. Within the first few paragraphs, the reader should know what you are attempting to predict, explain, interpret, understand, or criticize.

❖ DO YOUR HOMEWORK

Your mother's favorite injunction remains inescapable, even though you have left the nest. Many a scholar in other disciplines has had an "inspired revelation" about the need to study communication phenomena, only to discover, red-faced, that an entire discipline devoted to its study has existed for centuries. If you wish to avoid the same embarrassment, you will carefully research the extant literature not just in communication but also in related fields to determine if your insights are in fact new and unique or you are tilling ground that has been thoroughly hoed before. The payoffs for such spadework, in addition to avoiding the work of reinventing the wheel, are that you may uncover relevant theorizing and findings that bolster or redirect your own thinking and that allow you the luxury of building on the shoulders of others rather than starting from the ground up. The discovery that someone in an entirely different arena has been thinking along the same lines as you can be as exciting as the original discovery of the idea itself (assuming that you are more motivated by the pursuit of knowledge than the pursuit of personal fame), because the convergence of ideas from different perspectives and databases serves as important validation of our own thinking. It also means that you may have a much larger audience for your own work if you can show how it relates to parallel lines of inquiry.

❖ DEFINE YOUR TERMS

When we become intimately familiar with an area, we tend to forget that others are far less familiar with it and that even seemingly obvious concepts may be foreign to them. Two types of definitions need to be distinguished—those that are constitutive or conceptual, and those that are operational. The former are the formal definitions of terms in your theory, and they should be sufficiently concise and precise so that the reader knows both what is included or excluded by your definitions and how they differ from seemingly related or synonymous concepts. In many cases, the terminology may differ across disciplines, but the concepts are in fact the same. In other cases, they may be similar but not identical to what you are discussing. Be explicit about the similarities and differences, and do not rely on lay understandings, which may be hopelessly vague and perhaps entirely off the mark, for the key terms in your theory.

The latter type of definition—operational—refers to the ways in which you plan to instantiate empirically the conceptual elements in your theory. Although the theory itself should be articulated in conceptual, not operational, terms (just as properly worded hypotheses should be posed in conceptual, not operational, terms), each conceptual term should have corresponding ways of being measured and should be amenable to multiple forms of measurement. If you are theorizing, for instance, about communication goals, you may have a variety of ways in which you might empirically test their impact, such as employing individuals' self-reported priorities in a given communication event. However, the theory itself is about goals and should be worded using such terminology.

At some point, your theoretical concepts will be defined in terms of yet other concepts that must remain undefined if you are to avoid an infinite regress. These undefined terms are left as "primitives" in your particular theory. That is not to say they will not be constitutively defined in someone else's theory, only that in your theory, they are the starting place for your own definitions. So, for example, goals may be primitive in one person's theory, but constitutively defined in another person's theory. It all depends on what the central focus of your work is and which concepts are critical to understanding your thinking.

❖ IDENTIFY YOUR ASSUMPTIONS

Identifying your assumptions is a stage that scholars often skip, yet it is crucial to understanding what perspectives and assumptions you are importing into your theory or at least undergird it. For example, do you think communicators tend to be highly conscious, rational, and deliberate in their behavior, or do you subscribe to a view of humans as frequently operating on "automatic pilot," committing mindless, irrational, and/or spontaneous rather than thoughtful actions? Do you think the degree of voluntary, intentional, and planned action is contingent on specifiable conditions? More to the point, do issues of consciousness, intentionality, instinctiveness, and automaticity have any relevance to your theory? Do you think that affect plays a role comparable to that of cognition in governing human behavior? Do you favor a more biologically based or sociologically based view of human behavior? Do you see human action from a systems perspective? Are there particular meta-theoretical positions that guide your thinking? Are there theories from other disciplines that you are incorporating and that function themselves as primitives in your theory?

Returning to my own work as an example, when my colleagues and I were first developing nonverbal expectancy violations theory, I came to realize that I was influenced strongly by a number of psychological and biological theories related to human responsiveness to novel and arousing stimuli. At the same time, I was utilizing sociological principles of norms and expectations. I was also drawing upon a behaviorist perspective on the role of rewards in reinforcing, intensifying, diminishing, or extinguishing certain communicative responses. It was important that I make explicit, if only for myself (but preferably also for readers), what assumptions I was making so that I could determine if they were incompatible with one another and reconcile any conflicts.

Because communication as a discipline draws upon the knowledge bases of so many other disciplines, it is easy to fall into the trap of treating the profusion of theories that abound across allied disciplines like a Chinese menu in which you can pick one item from Column A, another from Column B, and so forth. To do so, however, often signals only the most superficial understanding of the theories, because they each have embedded in them their own assumptions about knowledge, human nature, and communication, some or many of which may conflict with one another. It is therefore a very useful preliminary exercise to identify your currently held assumptions and how they figure into your theorizing in either a tacit or explicit manner. Then state what those assumptions are in your writings.

❖ DETERMINE AT WHAT LEVEL YOUR THEORY IS PITCHED

Although it is universally recognized that we will never develop a unified theory of communication and that the pursuit of a single theory would be folly, there are strong differences of opinion as to whether midrange theories (ones of fairly large scope) are even possible. Many feel that a theory must be built around a single explanatory mechanism, a single variable or process that accounts for the observed phenomenon of interest (e.g., arousal, hedonic tone, heuristic information processing, need hierarchies, biological imperatives, intolerance for uncertainty, or universal politeness norms). If no explanatory mechanism is offered, or there are multiple explanatory factors, some would consider that what is being advanced is not a theory at all. This is perhaps why so many "models" rather than theories abound. Models escape the requirement of specifying unitary causes and, indeed, usually specify a large number of linkages. Nonetheless, these are theories in that they specify which communication-relevant variables relate to one another and how they do so.

I do not happen to agree that a theory needs to be so microscopic that it can safely revolve around a single explanatory variable. The theories to which I have devoted some considerable effort developing and testing have been midrange theories, which is to say they are neither simple nor small. Some would say that is one of their failings—that they lack parsimony and elegance. It is true that all else being equal, simpler is better. I do not buy the notion that our job as communication scholars is to "complexify" rather than simplify. However, for me (and apparently for many other communication scholars), communication processes do not admit to simple and easy explanations unless one has carved out a project of rather narrow scope. Even then, one may still have to reconcile how a particular explanatory mechanism relates to explanations being proffered outside the narrow confines of the theory. For example, scholars working on cognitive explanations are now constantly being pressed to address how their theories take account of affective or instinctive or physiological variables.

That said, there is virtue in not proposing a model or theory of such magnitude—a "one size fits all" approach—that it defies comprehension or cannot be subjected to adequate testing and possible falsification. In fact, larger theories, like oak trees, from smaller "acorn" theories grow. Therefore, starting smaller and letting the work evolve into something larger makes a great deal of sense.

All the things I have proposed so far are just the preliminaries to articulating the main arguments of the theory itself. At this stage, there are many different treatises on what the theory should look like, what its principal ingredients need be, and how they should be put together. It is probably advisable at this juncture to consult such writings so that you are consistent in your terminology, know what kind of theorizing you are doing, and know what kinds of criteria are likely to be applied to your work by your target audience. What a critical theorist expects to see, for example, is going to be different from what a social constructivist or logical positivist expects to see. In fact, there is considerable controversy surrounding whether the traditional conventions and criteria of social science—replicability, objectivity, falsifiability, parsimony, and accretion of knowledge, for example—even remain valid.

What follows as my final bits of advice are thus necessarily shaped by my own philosophy of science and my own efforts to create empirically testable social scientific theory. They represent the steps my colleagues and I have followed in our own theorizing, and are therefore only one way to go about the process. Perhaps they will at least serve as a concrete illustration of how to go about laying out a theoretical essay and have some applicability beyond my own brand of social science.

❖ SPECIFY PROPOSITIONS OR AXIOMS TO CREATE A LOGICAL PROGRESSION OF ARGUMENTS

Theorizing is a rhetorical activity. It is your job to create a convincing case for your position, whether you are proposing a causal model, offering a new interpretive framework, or advancing a particular critique. When I speak of propositions or axioms, I am referring to the central claims for which you must then provide warrants and evidence. If you are going to avoid fuzzy thinking and to create a logically related set of arguments, you need to make them explicit for yourself first, and then analyze them critically to see if they create internal contradictions, conflict with your assumptions, omit critical aspects of your argument, and cohere into an understandable account of some aspect of human behavior.

This is not to say that the theory needs to be complete. You can demur from trying to address everything at once and carve out some subset of the larger problem to be addressed. For example, scholars trying to understand why people are so poor at detecting deception have come at the problem from many different directions, such as how receivers process social information. Even within that general information-processing perspective, a host of different explanations have been offered (e.g., hypotheses related to truth bias, distraction, familiarity, accommodation to senders' intentional cues, visual biases, cognitive biases, cognitive busyness, and self-persuasion), each of which might be called its own "theory," because each posits its own explanatory mechanism for why deceivers are so successful.

Once you have created your skeletal list of propositional statements, try to order them in a logical and coherent progression (something akin to a legal brief or debate case). This will inevitably require much rearranging, addition of new statements, and integration or deletion of yet other statements. Then, see if you can dispense with any of the statements and still have a sensible theory. This is often the point at which you will expose fuzzy thinking, unnecessary terms in your theory, contradictory or inconsistent claims, missing links, and assumptions that have yet to be thought through. For example, nonverbal expectancy violations theory originally included arousal as a key element. In subsequent modifications, we came to realize that it was not so much arousal that was so relevant as it was the possible attentional shifts caused by violations, irrespective of whether they were accompanied by physiological arousal changes. This is but one small example of the innumerable changes your theory is likely to undergo once you have spelled out your current framework.

As with building a house, erecting the frame is still a long way from having a finished edifice. The statements are just the supports to which must be added supportive evidence and reasoning. Assumptions, although articulated at the outset, should be interjected along the way as the warrants for your claims. Like mortar between the evidentiary bricks, they serve to bind everything together and make what you hope will be a compelling case. At this stage of assembling all the parts, including insertion of relevant work by other authors, you may again find flaws in your thinking or find that what you are proposing conflicts with extant data. This is yet another opportunity to revise your thinking.

Finally, consider how you might go about testing the theory. Propose hypotheses that emanate from the propositions and possible means of operationalizing those terms that are not hypothetical constructs. If this last exercise does not uncover heretofore-overlooked problems, and you do not intend to test the theory yourself first, you are ready to release it for public consumption.

❖ REFERENCE

Kaplan, A. (1964). *Conduct of inquiry: Methodology for behavioral science.* San Francisco: Chandler.

5

The Challenge of
Writing the Quantitative Study

Alan M. Rubin

❖ ❖ ❖

All research begins with a problem that we need to solve. That problem may involve facilitating interpersonal interactions among people, increasing productivity in groups or organizations, improving the effectiveness of public communication, assessing the effects of televised violence or of Internet pornography on children, or any number of similar communication concerns. The major focus of this chapter will be on the challenges of preparing an effective quantitative research study.

AUTHOR'S NOTE: The author appreciates the input of several colleagues, all members of the editorial board of the *Journal of Communication*, who responded to a request for key tips to prospective authors: Charles Bantz, Charles Berger, Claude-Jean Bertrand, Franklin Boster, Douglas Boyd, James Bradac, Donald Browne, Akiba Cohen, Joseph Dominick, Don Ellis, Douglas Gomery, Bradley Greenberg, Pat Kearney, Dafna Lemish, Roy Moore, Richard Perloff, Michael Pfau, Ronald Rice, Karl Erik Rosengren, Rebecca Rubin, Michael Salwen, Nancy Signorielli, Leslie Steeves, Robert Stevenson, Joseph Turow, Barbara Wilson, Mike Wirth, and Kyu Ho Youm.

However, it is the research problem, rather than the quantitative or qualitative nature of the data we have collected, that is the driving force behind the research study and the manuscript. Nevertheless, throughout the chapter I will identify directions to take, and hazards to avoid, to prepare successful research manuscripts.

The act of writing any manuscript is rhetorical in nature, whether the problem is theoretical—such as explaining the worth of a model of intercultural competence—or applied—such as increasing group satisfaction. Theory, though, transcends the individual case at hand and helps us explain regularities in behavior across different settings and times. To be most beneficial, solving applied problems also should be guided by theory. Our goal in writing about a research problem is to persuade our audience that what we write is meaningful, useful, and interesting.

To prosper, a manuscript must survive the initial scrutiny of an editor and a set of reviewers. To increase our chances of success, we need to follow the journal's conventions for submitting our work and for meeting the expectations of what should be included in a solid analysis of a problem. In a creative and interesting manner, we must convince our audience that what we present is theoretically meaningful, fills important gaps in our knowledge, and is methodologically and analytically sound.

❖ THE RESEARCH PROBLEM

Too often, the quantitative analysis of a research problem is driven by the data we have collected or our statistical analysis of those data. Such efforts are typically referred to as "scientizing," because our focus is on creative analysis of the data rather than careful and systematic development and analysis of ideas. Too often, we plan our method for collecting or accessing the data before we know *why* we are collecting the data. The data and the method are the wrong places to begin a research study. We need to start with the research problem and a well-conceived plan for developing and analyzing the problem.

The research problem needs to be significant, relevant, and interesting. Too often, we take this for granted. Unfortunately, this is not always as obvious to our readers as it is to us. Our initial task in writing about our research problem—whether our research venture is quantitative, qualitative, or triangulated—is quite straightforward. We must make it clear to our readers why they should read past the first few pages of the paper.

When we write about a quantitative research study, we must accomplish several goals in the paper's introduction. We need to (a) identify and explain a unique and interesting problem, (b) focus the investigation on that problem, (c) establish the problem's theoretical meaning and relevance, (d) justify the problem's significance and present a rationale for study, and (e) discover and synthesize what others have written before about related issues, and where the gaps in our knowledge about the problem lie. We must devote substantial energy to accomplishing this multifaceted task.

Interesting and Important

Initially, we must identify and explain why the problem we are investigating is interesting and important. We must articulate our justification for doing the work and explain why someone should want to read the paper. Our research must be interesting, not just to ourselves, but also to others who read it. Therefore, very early in the manuscript we should (a) explain the importance of our study, (b) provide a conceptual framework for the investigation so that findings are meaningful beyond the present case study, and (c) explain why someone should even care about the study and its findings.

Our rationale for doing the research must focus on the importance of the problem we are studying. For example, if we want to study how the cellular telephone helps people stay interpersonally connected, we first need to search the communication and related literature about the social uses of the telephone. We want to see what others have done and written before our project. Gaps, omissions, or inconsistencies in the literature may help establish a basis for our work. That is, they might provide us with a solid rationale for conducting our study. Overall, though, our mission in searching the literature and writing the literature review is to place our study within the context of what we do and do not know about the research problem.

The literature review should provide a balanced portrait of our current state of knowledge about the research problem. It should lead to the derivation of precise research questions and testable hypotheses. In writing the review and critiquing the past research, though, we should avoid self-serving, gratuitous criticisms of others' work (and self-serving praise of our own previous work). We need to keep the research problem, literature review, and hypotheses focused on each other. Again, it is the problem and not the data that drives the study.

When we shift our inquiry from the utility of one communication medium, such as television, to another medium, such as satellite television, computers, or digital video devices, we should not simply assume that the research is interesting, important, and conceptually meaningful just because we are studying a newer medium or device. We must devote serious thought and explanation to suggest why studying people's use of this newer medium warrants scrutiny and is interesting and meaningful beyond our own study and sample. In the first page or two of the manuscript, we must explain the value of the work to those who read it. So, we begin with an interesting and important problem, and then carefully develop our arguments to build on the earlier published work of other authors and to justify the problem's significance and underlying theoretical framework.

Conceptual Framework

Our guiding theoretical framework is important because it leads us to ask relevant questions, make appropriate predictions, and have some basis for interpreting the results. The theory should lead to compatible and precise statements of research questions and testable hypotheses to guide the method and analysis of the study. For example, if we examine the prevalence or effects of violent or sexual content on television or the Internet, we should frame our problem so that an appropriate theory— whether it is social cognition, priming, cultivation, catharsis, mood management, or uses and gratifications—helps guide the questions we ask and the predictions we make. Eventually, that theory also will help us explain our results.

Initially, our guiding theory helps frame our questions. For example, do viewers imitate the behaviors of aggressive models or characters they see on television (social cognition)? Or, do aggressive portrayals cue viewers' responses (priming)? Or, do viewers develop perceptions of their environment based on the depiction of televised images (cultivation)? Or, does watching violent images purge viewers' aggressive tendencies (catharsis)? Or, do consumers choose Internet content to manage their moods or emotions (mood management)? Or, do personality differences or social circumstances lead to different motives for using the Internet (uses and gratifications)?

Each of these questions illustrates a different conceptual perspective about our research problem. Each also leads to different predictions or expectations. One prediction might be that more frequent participation in Internet chat rooms produces greater feelings of social isolation. An alternate prediction, depending on our theoretical perspective, might be that those who are socially isolated tend to participate more often in Internet chat rooms than those who are socially integrated. A different prediction might be that trait aggression and arousal predict selection of and exposure to violent programs on television. An alternate prediction might be that those who tend to watch violent content on television become aroused and aggressive.

Therefore, to conduct our quantitative study, we begin with a problem. Our understanding of—and expectation about—the problem is guided by a theory of human behavior. That theory leads to specific hypotheses or research questions to explore relationships among relevant concepts. These hypotheses guide how we gather our empirical data and suggest what statistical tests are appropriate for analyzing the data. Those who read and evaluate what we write about our research studies look for close and logical links among the research problem, theory, hypotheses or research questions, data, statistical analysis, and interpretation. In short, the conceptual framework suggests how we approach our study, and further makes the data and results more meaningful and interpretable beyond the single study.

Focus

We also must focus our study. This is not always easy to do. For example, it is no easy task for a young researcher to condense a 200-page dissertation in a 30-page article. It often is necessary to divide a dissertation into two or three separate articles based on different goals or purposes. Whether it is a dissertation, thesis, grant report, or research study, we should not attempt more than we can comfortably accomplish in one article. Do not try to address every element of the dissertation in a single article. Doing so is simply impractical and destined to fail. Instead, focus on one important, interesting problem. The hypotheses and research questions that emerge from our theory and literature review of the research problem, then, help focus our study and frame how we conduct the study and present our results.

In addition, there is room for exploratory research. However, once we progress beyond several related studies, editors and reviewers typically expect to see a study driven by specific predictions or research hypotheses derived from theory and tested in the study. Editors and reviewers often form strong preliminary judgments about the quality of the manuscript when reading the first few pages. It is therefore important to focus the paper quickly and to develop the research problem in a compelling and interesting manner. It also is important to make very clear how the hypotheses are logically derived from the literature, and to define clearly the key terms included in the hypotheses. For example, what do we mean by *exposure* or *arousal* or *aggression*? We also must use terminology consistently throughout the manuscript.

Once we accomplish this crucial task of defining and developing an interesting and meaningful problem that leads to sound and testable hypotheses, there are some basic guidelines about method and presentation to keep in mind. These guidelines apply irrespective of the journal to which we submit our work.

❖ THE METHOD

Every research problem presents us with a series of choices about our sampling, design, procedure, measurement, and statistical analysis. We need to provide complete detail about the method we employ to answer the research questions or to test the hypotheses. Readers need to see how the method adequately addresses the hypotheses. They need to be convinced that we have made sensible choices and have taken steps that allow us to test our hypotheses or to answer our research questions in a meaningful way.

Authors, therefore, must provide readers with sufficient information about the sample, design, measurement, and analysis to judge the merits of the study and of the results presented. Replication is essential in scientific research. We must consider whether we have provided enough information about our method so that another investigator can replicate our work.

The Sample

Often, it is better to err on the side of too much detail than too little detail about the reasoning behind and description of our methodological choices. We may need additional detail to explain our choice of sample or design, or our decisions about measurement or analysis. For example, we may feel that a sample of college students is acceptable for our research. However, we know that a traditional sample of college students is not always desirable, because, although convenient, that sample may not be appropriate for the topic we are studying (e.g., television news viewing or voting behavior) and our ability to generalize from it to other populations may be questionable. Therefore, we need to explain and justify our choice of such a sample.

We might justify the sample by attending to the nature of the study or the questions we are asking, the relevance of that age group to what we are studying (e.g., examining the uses of popular music or of the Internet might actually benefit from such a targeted sample), the need to investigate hypothesized relationships in a manner similar to past studies, the need for efficient and economical data gathering, and the like. In addition, personality factors and many communication behaviors of college students may vary in a manner similar to broader populations. So, whereas a college student sample is not always desirable, it is possible to explain why it is a rational and logical choice for our study.

When writing about our study, then, we need to explain and justify how and why we selected the sample. We also need to provide some basic, descriptive information about the sample, including, at a minimum, age and gender distributions—for example, the percentages of men and women, the average age, and the range of ages. Other demographic descriptors, such as racial or ethnic sample composition, also may be relevant depending on what we are studying.

Sometimes we sample objects or artifacts, such as media content, instead of people. If we are doing a content analysis, we need to explain how we randomly selected our sample of media content in order to identify and count our units of analysis. For example, we would need to explain how we selected a stratified probability sample based on newspaper or magazine titles, or how we chose a systematic sample of top-100 songs to analyze lyrics, or how we constructed a composite week of television news programs.

Sampling, then, is one important choice. We must have a good and reasonable sample so that we can provide a fair and meaningful test of our hypotheses. Because much of what we write about a study is persuasive rather than just descriptive, we need to convince the reader that this is a good sample for considering the research problem.

Research Design

Besides sampling, research design is another important choice. We do not want to present to the reader what appears to be a fishing expedition in search of statistical significance. Instead, we want to explain a clear and systematic design or plan for our method and analysis. We must make it evident how we designed our study to allow us to test the hypotheses and answer the research questions. We need to explain how our design enabled both sufficient variation in what we are studying and control of extraneous factors.

If we manipulate our independent variable while maintaining tight control over extraneous factors, we will need to explain which experimental design we chose. For instance, if we examined whether level of frustration affects how adolescents respond to aggressive portrayals in televised music videos, we will need to explain how we manipulated the level of frustration of participants in an experimental condition while controlling for the age and gender of participants and their exposure to other televised portrayals. An experimental design may not provide the external validity we would like for some problems and questions, but it enables us to manipulate our independent variable in a desired manner and to achieve greater control over extraneous factors, if that is what we need in our study. When writing the paper, we should clearly explain, for example, why we selected a posttest only control group design instead of a pretest-posttest control group design (perhaps to avoid sensitizing our subjects), or why sacrificing the external validity of a field experiment provided us with better internal validity (owing to tighter controls over possible extraneous factors).

However, if we need to examine associations among our variables, a correlation design may be sufficient. In that instance, we might need to explain how we provided appropriate controls for possible confounding variables in the statistical analysis—for example, by controlling for the perceived realism of television content when examining links between television exposure and cultivation effects.

Our research design, then, must provide a good and fair test of theoretically informed hypotheses. How it does that must be clear in our presentation. We may need to explain, for instance, how the design restricted, as much as possible, Type I or Type II errors from occurring. Alternatively, we may need to address how the design allowed us to find meaningful and significant differences or associations among our variables if—and only if—they actually exist. We should be able to explain how our method and design allowed us to lay out an efficient and systematic route to achieve the most sensible choices in design, measurement, and analysis.

Measurement

Our choices must closely reflect the independent and dependent variables specified in the hypotheses and research questions. We need to explain to our readers how the measures we designed, adapted, and used validly and reliably reflected the concepts specified in the hypotheses or research questions. Perhaps we have established the *content validity* of a measure by assessing its dimensionality in a factor analysis (e.g., finding that a measure of competence contains skill, knowledge, and motivation dimensions), or we supported its *criterion-related validity* by linking the measure to related measures (e.g., comparing a new measure of listening comprehension to previous measures of listening), or we established its *construct validity* by tapping the meaning of a construct (e.g., by linking a measure of frustration to a propensity to be aggressive).

Authors also must make it clear to the reader how our operationalization matches our conceptualization. That is, we must make a strong case for *ecological validity*. In other words, we may need to devote a few sentences to show how our measures—as reflected, for example, in the survey questions we ask or in the observations or experimental manipulation we employ—truly represent our constructs, whether we are studying aggression, apprehension, arousal, communication competence, communication satisfaction, group productivity, interpersonal attraction, media dependency, motivation, perceived realism, television exposure, or violence.

Authors must make the process of building or using valid and reliable measures clear to the readers. For example, as researchers we need to work at improving the *reliability* of a measure by fine-tuning the items we choose to include in a measurement index, such as by eliminating 2 of the 20 statements that lower the Cronbach *alpha* reliability coefficient for an index of the Felt Importance of the Internet. If we do not have strong evidence for the reliability of scaled measures—for example, Cronbach alphas above a minimal .60— then we need to go back to our printouts to identify unreliable items that need to be dropped or reworded, or we go back to the literature to help refine items to achieve that higher level of reliability.

We must also explain to the reader, often in a condensed fashion, how we pilot and pretest our measures to help improve their validity and reliability, for instance explaining how we refined the wording of questionnaire items to reflect the construct more accurately and precisely. Also, measures do not necessarily perform the same way when we adapt them for a purpose other than that for which they were originally intended or if we use them in a culture different from where they were developed. If we are using a measure differently, we often need to pretest either newly developed or adapted measures and, again, note this in the manuscript. Consequently, in our manuscripts, we must explain succinctly to the readers how we went about establishing validity and reliability for the measures we are using in our study.

Validity Questions

Clearly, then, we need to address the validity and reliability of our measures. Reviewers rightfully regard measurement invalidity as a fatal flaw in a study. Although our writings seldom do a sufficient job establishing the validity of measurement, authors sometimes address content- and construct-validity issues via the presentation of a content analysis. However slight the treatment may be for issues relating to validity, authors should present support for measurement validity and reliability in the method section of a manuscript. Here are a series of questions to consider addressing, depending on what we actually are doing in the study and how much space may be available in the typical article published in the journal to which we are submitting the manuscript:

- What do prior literature and past use tell us about the measure's validity and reliability? Does the measure have an established track record of validity and reliability to support its application?
- Have we adequately addressed content validity in the current study? Does the measure reflect the multifaceted or multidimensional nature of the construct? Is there, for example, more than a single dimension of perceived realism when examining attitudes toward media content, or of parasocial relationships with media personalities?

- Have we sufficiently addressed criterion-related and construct validity? Does an index of political participation actually predict the likelihood that someone will vote or be attuned to political news in the media?
- Does the measure truly represent the construct being studied? Do our paper-and-pencil measures of aggression, motivation, exposure, and the like reflect the conceptual meaning of these constructs? Do single- or multiple-item indexes of satisfaction truly address consumer satisfaction with a product or a participant's satisfaction with a communication encounter or relationship?
- If the measure was developed in a different context, for a different purpose, or in a different culture, is it appropriate for our investigation? For example, can we adequately assess cultivation's mean-world beliefs with Rosenberg's Faith in People Scale? Would Hofstede's measure of cultural value dimensions be appropriate for our study?

Reliability Questions

Besides such questions and issues about measurement validity, we must also consider and clearly present evidence of the reliability of the measure. Here are several questions to consider:

- Should we account for the measure's stability over time? Yes, and researchers sometimes do so with test-retest correlations.
- Do we have sufficient coder agreement in a content or interaction analysis? Even if coders agree 85% of the time, they still disagree 15% of the time; therefore, there always is a degree of error in such research.
- How do we resolve discrepancies between coders? Typically, we may ask coders to discuss their disagreement after the fact to arrive at a common decision. Alternatively, the researcher (who did not participate in the coding) resolves the discrepancy.
- Is a single-item measure sufficient to explain and establish homogeneity and dependability of measurement? It probably is not, although single-item measures may be used in large-scale telephone surveys. Sometimes, researchers sacrifice reliability or even measurement precision (e.g., having fewer finite response options or points on a scale) for the opportunity of securing a large random sample for their study.
- How low is too low for a Cronbach alpha measure of homogeneity? We certainly should not rely on measures with alphas below .60; yet even then there is already a substantial amount of unaccounted-for error in that relationship. We can increase alpha by deleting items with low item-total correlations, by adding related items, and by improving the wording of some items in a pilot investigation.

❖ THE RESULTS

Statistical Analysis

It is important for readers to know the statistical techniques that we use and to understand the measurement needs, application, and reporting requirements of those techniques. Any deviations from that proper application and use of a statistical technique when we report our results will raise serious concerns on the part of the reviewers and editor. Researchers need to match their statistical techniques with the requirements of the different levels of measurement for their independent and dependent variables. Our levels of measurement determine whether we have continuous or discrete data, and establish which statistical tests might be appropriate to test those data. For example, if our independent variable is categorical (such as a preferred mass medium) and our dependent variable is continuous (such as knowledge of political affairs), then an analysis of variance would be an appropriate test. However, if we have multiple dependent variables that are conceptually and methodologically correlated (such as a knowledge of political affairs or interest in politics) to go along with that categorical independent variable, we need to use a multivariate analysis of variance before—or instead of—considering separate relationships for each dependent measure.

We also must be able to explain and justify whenever we use statistical tests in a manner that deviates from standard statistical expectations or requirements, such as if we were to dummy code gender as "0" for male and "1" for female, or to use an ordinal measurement for media exposure (e.g., *often, sometimes, never*) in a correlation or regression analysis.

It also should be obvious in our presentation how our choice of statistical procedure aligns with the needed test of relationship implied in our hypothesis. Certain statistics present us with measures of association—such as correlation, regression, and canonical correlation—and others with measures of differences. Analysis of variance, for example, is appropriate for examining curvilinear differences among groups, but is less appropriate for examining linear relationships among continuous antecedent and consequent constructs.

Therefore, our statistics need to match the levels of measurement of our constructs. They also must be appropriate for the types of relationships specified in our hypotheses and research questions. Finally, this must be clearly presented to our readers.

Let us assume that our hypothesis follows a conceptual model specifying how certain constructs (age, viewing motivation, and liking a character) entered into the equation in a predetermined order will predict the amount of television exposure. The hypothesis probably calls for a regression analysis and, because it specifies a conceptual order, most likely a hierarchical regression analysis. Regression analysis requires us to examine the relative contributions of each independent variable when we enter it into the equation to try to explain and predict television exposure. We also must control for relevant extraneous factors, when needed. For the regression, we would need to report beta weights for the contributions of each predictor variable to the overall equation, percentages of variance explained at each step of the regression, and the significance of the change in F at each step of the regression.

Data Presentation

It is important to consider how statistical data should be presented in the text and tables of a manuscript. All statistical results should be presented in an organized and systematic fashion. Usually, they follow the same sequence as the hypotheses and research questions. In addition, all statistical presentations must provide the correct statistics and summary data for the analyses used. This is true whether we use univariate or more complex multivariate analyses. It also is wise to examine recent issues of the journal to which we intend to send our work to see how the editor treats data in the text and tables.

We must take extraordinary care with how we collect, code, and analyze our data. A researcher can rest assured that any carelessness in data collection or presentation will cause the reader to question seriously the veracity of the data and the worth of the manuscript. We must report all data accurately and precisely; that is, without errors in observation, calculation, or reporting. This is true for quantitative and qualitative research, whether we are presenting the results of an experiment, survey, content analysis, field observation, or ethnography. Errors in presentation in the manuscript call negative attention to our data; if we make mistakes in presenting the data, reviewers often will think we also made mistakes when collecting and analyzing our data.

We must report quantitative data precisely. This includes providing the necessary descriptive statistics for scales and measures, such as means and standard deviations, which we round to the appropriate number of decimal places (usually one or two) for the journal to which we submit our work. There should be no fudging as to the meaning of results. To say, for example, that data only "approach statistical significance" is to say that they actually are *not* significant: Why should we suggest otherwise when we write the manuscript? If our participants watched 2.4 hours of television yesterday, we should say that, precisely, and not that they watched "a couple of hours."

We also must be honest and accurate when we report results. For example, a .20 correlation does *not* suggest a strong relationship, even if the correlation is significant at the $p < .001$ level. Large sample sizes cause relatively small correlations to be statistically significant. It would be accurate and prudent to suggest that the strength of such a relationship is not substantial, even if it is statistically significant.

We should identify the appropriate statistical technique and report the required information for that statistic. For factor analysis, for example, we should choose the correct mode of analysis and rotation of the factors, and report eigenvalues and percentage of variance explained after rotation. Again, these figures should be rounded to one or two decimal places, depending on the journal's practices. We also should report primary and relevant secondary loadings, how indexes are computed from the factors, and what the reliabilities are—for example, Cronbach alphas for each index that are computed from factor loadings or factor scores. Furthermore, we need to report the rules that we followed to retain items and factors—saying, for example, that to be retained a factor needs to have at least two items that load at .60 or higher on the primary factor and under .40 on any secondary factor. We should clearly describe and explain these choices to our readers.

Some journals also require specific statistical conventions, such as strength of association and power statistics for significant or nonsignificant relationships. Some have precise styles to follow when presenting statistical tests, even down to the number of decimals to report, usually one or two places. What is beyond that second decimal place of a *t*-test, an *F*, or an *r* does not matter much in communication research. Besides being a sure sign of a novice researcher, extending the decimal places to four or five places, or even to as far as the computer printout goes, interferes with effective communication. All meaningful probability levels can be reported with two or three decimal positions. Is it really meaningful if we report $p < .0001$ or $.00001$ instead of $p < .001$? Read some recent articles in the appropriate journal, and follow that journal's practices exactly. Again, do not invite reviewers to get so caught up in statistical minutia or in stylistic violations and omissions that they lose sight of the value and contributions of the work.

Journals and chapters do not always allow sufficient space for including all necessary details. We need to check both the journal's submission information and recent articles published in the journal to discover the editor's expectations and requirements. We must include what is needed, and provide a note as to how the reader can obtain further information about the procedures, measures, and analyses if space does not allow for their inclusion in the article (e.g., we might write that the complete factor matrix is available from the senior author, or that the content coding scheme is available from the first author). In initial submissions, err on the side of too much detail and information, which can always be trimmed if that is what the editor wants in a revised paper. Anticipate the areas of concern, and provide sufficient explanation for what you think an editor or reviewer might question.

Tabular Presentation

Typically, we report most data in the text and keep the number of tables to a minimum. However, a few tables or figures can be useful for visually summarizing important information. Tables and figures must be clearly presented and uncluttered. Identify each table with a precise title that appropriately describes its content and function. We also must clearly label rows and columns in tables, and include precise, relevant data, whether they be raw scores, means, percentages, numbers of cases, or the like.

Make certain that all data in the text and tables are correct. Check that columns and rows add up correctly and that percentages sum to 100% (perhaps 99.9% or 100.1%, if rounded). Redundancy across the text and tables is typically discouraged. However, if the same data are in the text and tables, make sure they agree. If they do not, the reviewer will, at a minimum, be confused and frustrated by the presentation. In addition, use table notes to report statistical differences or associations—especially

if they are not included in the text—and to provide clear, precise explanations for anything that may be confusing in the tables or in need of
clarification.

In addition, make certain that all statistical presentations adhere to
the content and stylistic requirements of the journal. We must provide the
appropriate statistics required by the periodical to which we submit our
manuscript, whether that publication follows the style of the American
Psychological Association (i.e., APA style; American Psychological Association, 1994), the Modern Language Association (i.e., MLA style;
Gibaldi, 1995), or another style (e.g., *The Chicago Manual of Style*, 1993).
The manuals contain solid and essential information, ranging from statistics to grammar to organization. Keep the appropriate manual handy and
follow it religiously. Do not encourage the reviewers to be distracted by
stylistic miscues.

❖ THE DISCUSSION

Discussion sections of research articles should do more than just repeat
the results for each hypothesis or research question. By the time the
reader reaches the discussion, he or she knows what the results *are*. Although a capsule summary of the important findings is useful after a
complex analysis, our purpose when writing the discussion is not to
leave the meaning and implications of the results to chance or the interpretation of the results to the reader. Our purpose in the discussion is to
tell the reader what the results *mean* and why they matter.

The discussion should remind the reader how the study has delivered
what we promised up front. It also should integrate the study's findings
with the theory that we proposed to use to guide the investigation in the
introduction. In the discussion, we also should tell why the findings are
meaningful in a practical sense, and point to needed future directions.

Consider addressing several questions in the discussion:

- What is the significance of the information found in the study? Of what
  value are the results to the reader? What is the contribution of the findings to knowledge and practice?
- What bearing do the results have on the underlying theory? Do the results support the theory, or do they suggest some rival explanation?
  What explanations might exist for unexpected or contradictory findings?

- What are the study's major limitations? What different paths might researchers follow in the future?
- What do the procedures and findings suggest for future inquiries?

We should not be shy about suggesting what the study's limitations are. All research studies have limitations. Editors and reviewers appreciate a clear and honest recognition and explication of these limitations. They also want to see an indication that we have thought about where the results lead us for future investigations.

❖ MANUSCRIPT PREPARATION

Work loses credibility if it is sloppy; that is, if it contains grammatical, typographical, or stylistic errors. We emphasize this point in a chapter titled "Writing Research Papers" in *Communication Research: Strategies and Sources* (Rubin, Rubin, & Piele, 2000). Good, clear, and concise writing is vital. This includes the need for precise and gender-neutral language, correct tense and subject agreement, active voice, effective transitions, solid paragraphs, good organization, and proper use of quotations and citations. Plagiarism will not and should not be tolerated. Paragraphs need to develop and support precise thesis statements or arguments. As Sternberg (1992) suggests, "An article tells a story. Like a story, it captures readers' interest. . . . Write for the reader, not for yourself. Readers appreciate the effort to keep their interest" (p. 13).

Use the available computer-assisted tools to check the paper's spelling and grammar. However, it also is vital that we carefully proofread our work and not depend on computer spell checkers to locate errors. Spell checkers do not catch misused words that are spelled correctly (e.g., *effect* vs. *affect, two* vs. *too*). The blind use of search-and-replace functions can cause disastrous results that cannot be corrected before submission unless we carefully proofread the work. I have seen instances where computers have changed parts of words and altered entries in the list of references because someone indiscriminately used the computer's search-and-replace function. Computer grammar and spell checkers also do not prevent missing pages, missing tables, incompatible dates between the text and references, incorrect data within tables, or missing, inaccurate, or incomplete references. The computer cannot accept blame for our carelessness: We, as writers, do. Furthermore, editors and reviewers are never encouraged by our carelessness.

It is essential that we check, recheck, edit, and rewrite all our work carefully several times before submitting it. If we are careless when preparing our manuscript, our credibility will suffer, and the reviewers will sense that we were careless when we collected, coded, analyzed, and presented our data. The editor and reviewers will question the worth of the manuscript.

Journals typically maintain high standards of effective presentation and consistency. It is important to follow the journal's accepted stylistic and bibliographic format. Some communication journals allow MLA style, yet most require APA style. Do not be bashful about consulting appropriate manuscript preparation and submission sources (e.g., Day, 1998; Dyer, 1999; Knapp & Daly, 1993), as well as grammar and writing sources (e.g., Kessler & McDonald, 1996; Strunk & White, 1979).

❖ CONCLUSION

In *Communication Research: Strategies and Sources* (Rubin, Rubin, & Piele, 2000), we note that accomplishing several things will bolster the chances of a successful outcome for a submitted manuscript. I have echoed and expanded upon many similar points in this chapter:

- *Provide an adequate rationale.* The purpose of the research should be clear very early in the paper. Establish the study's rationale and significance. The author, not the reader, has the burden of proof. Be persuasive, not just descriptive, throughout.

- *Ask interesting questions.* Ask good, compelling, interesting questions. Demonstrate that you know the literature and that you are asking important and interesting questions that emerge from gaps in your understanding. Convince the readers why they should be interested in what you have to say.

- *Be systematic, and follow precise, valid, and reliable procedures.* Present a clear plan for the study, not a fishing expedition. Explain why the methods and measures are sound. Explain what you have done to ensue valid and reliable measurement of your constructs. Sloppiness in method, measurement, and presentation is never acceptable.

- *Use appropriate samples.* The study's purpose suggests an appropriate sample. The method and analysis suggest the appropriate sample size. Explain and justify convenience samples.

- *Apply correct analyses.* Analyze the data fully and appropriately. Report the summary data and analyses correctly, precisely, and in an organized fashion. If editors or reviewers ask for a sensible, revised analysis, do it before resubmitting.

- *Establish contributions to knowledge.* Explain how the work furthers understanding the problem studied and the theory developed. What are its theoretical and practical applications? What are its limitations and future directions?

- *Submit to an appropriate outlet.* Make certain the work is compatible with and in proper form for the right publication forum. Make certain you have followed all the conventions and requirements for submission to that publication.

Many of the ingredients for writing a successful quantitative research study are incorporated in this chapter. Be precise and interesting when writing about the study. Focus and keep the purpose and significance in sight. Show how you carefully built on the foundation of a sound sample, solid research design, valid and reliable measurement, and appropriate statistical analysis. Demonstrate the work's heuristic value. If you design and execute solid research and present it in an interesting and compelling manner, it has a good chance of being published.

❖ REFERENCES

American Psychological Association. (1994). *Publication manual of the American Psychological Association* (4th ed.). Washington, DC: Author.

The Chicago manual of style (14th ed.). (1983). Chicago: University of Chicago Press.

Day, R. A. (1998). *How to write and publish a scientific paper* (5th ed.). Cambridge: Cambridge University Press.

Dyer, C. (Ed.). (1999). *The Iowa guide: Scholarly journals in mass communication and related fields* (7th ed.). Thousand Oaks, CA: Sage.

Gibaldi, J. (1995). *MLA handbook for writers of research papers* (4th ed.). New York: Modern Language Association of America.

Kessler, L., & McDonald, D. (1996). *When words collide: A media writer's guide to grammar and style* (4th ed.). Belmont, CA: Wadsworth.

Knapp, M. L., & Daly, J. A. (1993). *A guide to publishing in scholarly communication journals* (2nd ed.). Austin, TX: International Communication Association.

Rubin, R. B., Rubin, A. M., & Piele, L. J. (2000). *Communication research: Strategies and sources* (5th ed.). Belmont, CA: Wadsworth.

Sternberg, R. J. (1992, September). How to win acceptance by psychology journals: 21 tips for better writing. *APS Observer*, pp. 12–13, 18.

Strunk, W., Jr., & White, E. B. (1979). *The elements of style* (3rd ed.). New York: Macmillan.

6

The Challenge of
Writing the Qualitative Study

Thomas R. Lindlof

❖ ❖ ❖

This chapter tours the principal challenges of writing qualitative studies in communication—specifically, those relying on field-based approaches in the ethnographic tradition. Like other kinds of empirical
reports, the qualitative study must argue logically about literature, design, and data, and make the case for significance in its area of inquiry.
However, qualitative studies pose special challenges of their own. The
need for authors to be keenly sensitive to the uses of language (e.g., the
languages of the people they have studied, the languages of the narratives they write) is certainly one of the most prominent of these challenges. Constraints of space prevent this chapter from providing all that

AUTHOR'S NOTE: Excerpts from Emotion labor at 911: A case study and theoretical critique by S. J. Tracy and K. Tracy, *Journal of Applied Communication Research, 26*, 390-411, re-
printed with permission of the National Communication Association.

you should know about writing qualitative research (see Golden-Biddle & Locke, 1997; Wolcott, 1990), but hopefully it will characterize some of the major choices and strategies that can set you on the path to practicing the craft and enjoying the process.

Most qualitative studies are based in the tradition of *cultural hermeneutics*, which "posits reality as a polysemic system of meanings that must be centered in improvised performances of both discourse (language in use) and action" (Anderson, 1996, p. 191). Central to this view are these epistemic warrants: that human beings collectively construct the meaningfulness of their world (including its material features); that it is impossible to speak, act, or theorize outside of cultural discourses; and that these constructions of meaning vary historically and across cultural systems. In short, the irreducible element in qualitative study is not the behavior or the neural event, but the semiotic act. Everything methodological and analytical builds upon acts of making/understanding meaning in their contexts of social interaction and cultural resource.

The main purpose of qualitative texts is to explicate the action and discourse observed in the field, and to invite readers to understand what it means to live in the scene under study. This aspect of the text, often known as a *thick description* (Geertz, 1973), presents detailed narratives of the ways by which the social actors make sense of their space, texts, artifacts, relationships, community, or history. Research texts also problematize this inscribed experience within concepts and issues pertinent to communication. That is, the researcher interprets social life through certain analytic frames, producing claims and conjectures that contribute to disciplinary conversations about communication practices.

Qualitative studies have long pedigrees in anthropology and sociology (Vidich & Lyman, 1994), but their arrival in communication is comparatively recent. Fortunately, many of the challenges that formerly beset qualitative researchers in communication have fallen by the wayside. Now, nearly all journals declare their theoretical and methodological diversity. For the most part, they practice what they advertise. Books of methodological and philosophical examination (Anderson, 1996; Lindlof & Taylor, forthcoming; Potter, 1996) are also part of the life support system for this emerging area. With their place at the discipline's table assured, the main publication challenge that qualitative researchers face is the same as any other author: Understanding how to write research effectively so that its contribution can be recognized by editors, referees, and readers.

❖ TRAVELING IN THE CITY OF JOURNALS

A crucial step in this journey is becoming savvy about the competitive world of journals. It is helpful to think of this publishing environment in the metaphor of a city. The city center consists of the disciplinary journals whose skyline is visible from every compass point of the metropolitan area. These journals—among them *Journal of Communication, Human Communication Research, Communication Research, Communication Monographs, Journalism & Mass Communication Quarterly,* and *Journal of Broadcasting & Electronic Media*—are authority-invoking institutions whose main role is to decide what passes as "significant" works of knowledge production. The standards of these high-circulation, low–acceptance rate venues dictate that they will carry weight in the high-stakes games of job searches, recruitment, tenure and promotion, funding applications, and so forth.

Observing the infrequent appearance of qualitative work in some of the disciplinary journals, you might think that they harbor an implicit bias against the interpretive paradigm. This assumption does not usually hold up to close scrutiny of actual editorial decisions. Editors have minimal control over the kinds of manuscripts that come in—a fact that accounts better than any other for perceived shortages in this or other categories of research. You can scan the editorial board for clues to the editor's vision and how receptive the current regime may be to your work. However, you should not try to infer too much from the board membership, because the journal's referee base is much larger than this list. What is undoubtedly true when you submit a manuscript to a disciplinary journal is that you will compete—not directly, but for scarce page space—with a great many nonqualitative submissions. This situation probably favors the qualitative study that engages a topic of widely acknowledged importance with ingenuity and rigor, and whose prose style passes an accessibility threshold so that nonspecialists can appreciate the substantive ideas.

Moving out from the city center, one encounters the urban neighborhoods, gentrified and otherwise, where the long-standing topical interests of the discipline lie. Though more narrowly targeted than the big "downtown" journals, these special-interest journals represent important traditions of scholarship and are clearly indispensable in the niches they serve. For example, *Critical Studies in Mass Communication* and *Text and Performance Quarterly,* sponsored by the National Communication

Association, provide outlets for critical and cultural media research and studies of communicative performance, respectively, and both of them are quite hospitable to qualitative studies. If you submit your ethnography to a journal that openly welcomes this line of work, you can expect it to be read by referees who can process, even appreciate, high levels of conceptual complexity and terminological specificity (you will notice I did not say "jargon").

Those virtues aside, the circulation of special-interest journals is smaller than their disciplinary counterparts, and the articles may not be cited as often. Citation data are often used, fairly or not, as tangible measures of a work's value. Connoisseurs of paradox will savor the notion that a disciplinary journal, only a fraction of whose subscribers read any given piece, is valued more highly in the academic marketplace than the specialty journal, whose close-knit community tends to read and respond more intensively. However, do not fear professional obscurity if you publish there: Scholarly reputations are regularly made on the basis of articles in special-interest journals that influence the thinking and subsequent work of peers worldwide.

Finally, we arrive at the city's edge, where venture capital of the intellectual kind incubates the newest journals. Here, we find journals that redefine and extend knowledge in a variety of ways. They may dedicate themselves to emerging developments in the world at large (e.g., *Television and New Media*), experiment with new methods of presentation and delivery (e.g., *Journal of Computer-Mediated Communication*), or offer fresh alternatives to the older disciplinary journals (e.g., *Journalism*). What may be of interest to prospective authors is that this frontier is usually friendlier to the sort of adventurous, boundary-spanning product for which qualitative research is often known. Their editorial boards are often made up of a younger cohort of active scholars who may be more willing to work patiently with authors whose studies show promise of becoming innovative contributions.

In addition to how well your manuscript fits with a journal's identity, you must also assess its literal fit with the journal's length stipulations, typically in the 20- to 30-page range. This is a key issue for qualitative authors, because a study of even modest complexity can produce notes running to the hundreds of pages. Most of this material will not be used directly in the published study, but rather serve as a substructure of raw data, analytic memos, site descriptions, participant profiles, artifact inventories, and so forth. The relatively few selections that find their way into the manuscript bear the burden of accounting for a version of cultural reality and how this knowledge was acquired and shaped by the author—in other words, referencing the substructure that lies beneath. The page limits that journals impose mean that you must be a model of writing efficiency. Unfortunately, this efficiency can sometimes exact a cost in terms of thinning out the dense, evocative descriptions on which the credibility of such work hangs.

One escape route from this dilemma is to opt out of the zoning restrictions of Journal City for the wide-open country of the book or monograph. However, even university presses face economic pressures of their own, and are adopting acquisitions strategies that do not always favor the interests of academic ethnographers. The more compelling reasons for putting your efforts into article publishing are that they are universally recognized as the breeding grounds for innovation. As a practical career matter, a strong record of refereed articles is the best thing a young scholar can do to accrue reputational capital and gain the solicitous attention of senior editors at major publishing houses (Morris, 1998). Article writing also cultivates the skills of cogent argumentation and economy of expression that prove useful if and when you decide to turn to long form writing.

❖ THEORIZING THE STUDY
AND INTRODUCING THE SCENE

Writing the opening sections of your article involves a three-fold task: (a) developing a theoretical argument for the significance of the study, (b) delineating the research problem, and (c) introducing the scene in which your research took place. Collectively, these three components justify the research enterprise and set up the reader's expectations for what the rest of the article will deliver. Nearly all qualitative studies feature these components, although the research itself may be done in a different order. That is, your curiosity may initially be piqued by a striking social scene, cultural event, or relational dilemma; you then begin to focus the research problem, starting with an interrogation of your own assumptions and knowledge of the phenomenon; finally, you study the extant literature that allows you to begin building the argument. For our purposes here, we will consider the components in the original order shown above.

To be truly useful to other scholars, your study should be grounded in the theoretical discourses of one or more intellectual traditions. Cultural hermeneutics concerns human interpretation processes in their contexts of production, including the relations of power and agency that enable meanings to circulate and inform action. Going outside this paradigm for a theoretical platform is risky business, even for experienced researchers. As an example, researchers of the cultivation effects of television arguably rely on the survey method because of the interest in people's quasi-statistical perceptions of their social world. Could there be an ethnography of cultivation effects? Conceivably, but only if such effects are reconceptualized in terms of action and discourse (e.g., a study of the privileged residents of a gated community). Substantial work would be required to translate a social-cognitive perspective into a framework that is sensitive to multiple, performed realities, and there is no guarantee that you will succeed.

Because the strong suit of qualitative research is theory (or concept) generation, theory is often an outcome, not a precursor, of a successful study. Thus, theorizing happens all along the course of a study. Many researchers also think of theory as a localized entity built from the situated motives, vocabularies, and "folk theory" of the folk themselves. For example, Paul Lichterman (1992) found that the self-help book readers he studied had developed their own theory for how these books are authored, produced, and marketed—that is, "an epistemological underpinning for participation in the thin culture of self-help psychology reading" (p. 432). It may take a while to figure out how a situated theory fits with general concepts of communication (Carbaugh & Hastings, 1992). However, by the time you sit down to write your article, it can be safely assumed that you have decided on the intellectual tradition, or the theory and concepts within that tradition, that allows you to explain the significance of the processes and events you have documented in the field.

Effective conceptualizations are achieved in several ways. Your readers should be introduced to the current thinking and findings in the areas of your investigation, including the best available explanations. Although literature reviews in quantitative articles tend to track the incremental advances in knowledge with a view toward developing theory with higher predictive power, qualitative studies tend to cite other qualitative studies in order to indicate the diversity of action or discourse in particular kinds of social worlds. The aim is not to predict better, but to understand more richly. In their study of call-takers at a 911 communication center, Tracy and Tracy (1998) introduce the concept of what they call "emotion labor." Initially, their discussion hinges on the ideas of an important theorist, Arlie Hochschild. The authors then go on to expand the scope, forms, and explanations of emotion labor by citing a multitude of other studies. This, of course, is a common textual strategy that locates the origin of a concept and demonstrates how it has become more complex, and possibly more powerful, through subsequent research.

Your command of the literature is also on display here. Journal referees will look at how completely and accurately you have interpreted a body of work. Novice authors sometimes "bulk up" their conceptualizations with long lists of citations as a way of proving their facile grasp of the literature. However, readers will be more impressed with your incisive usage of key works than your bibliographic abilities. Overly long citation lists are also aesthetically inelegant; taken to an extreme, they can be arterial blockages in your narrative flow.

Should you report conflicting literatures? Of course!—Particularly if you want to get the most out of your study and its findings, and if you want to convince readers of the value of its contribution. Placid fields of study are usually fields in which the important questions have been settled or been superseded by other ideas and fields. Fields marked by disagreement attract a great deal of research activity, perhaps because the stakes are higher and the rewards greater. Importantly, clashing perspectives and findings, as Eisenhardt (1989) points out, are opportunities to push the envelope of what we know:

> The juxtaposition of conflicting results forces researchers into a more creative, framebreaking mode of thinking than they might otherwise be able to achieve. The result can be deeper insight into both the emergent theory and the conflicting literature, as well as sharpening of the limits to generalizability of the focal research. (p. 544)

In the Tracy and Tracy (1998) study, for example, the authors' next move in the literature review is to introduce "two lines of work [that] pose challenges to Hochschild's conception of emotional labor" (p. 393). The two lines of work, respectively, question the assumption that faking emotions in the workplace is always harmful and propose that emotion suppression should be considered a form of emotion labor in some professional circumstances. These findings are pivotal to the theoretical argument, because they lead to the construction of the research questions underpinning their study.

The development of a theoretical argument is driven by a purpose: To show the reader why *this* world of scholarship we commonly inhabit would be changed for the better by an empirical exploration of *this* problem. In a very real sense, the author is telling a story—Act One of a four-act play, if you will—that should peak dramatically with the unveiling of the research problem. However, this is a dispassionate, logical kind of drama. The reader of your manuscript will not willingly suspend disbelief. If the theory is inappropriate, if the treatment of the literature is clumsy or incomplete, if the arguments do not bridge us adequately to the reason for the study, then you are unlikely to persuade informed readers of the soundness of the entire enterprise. In the parlance of editors and referees, you may have committed one or more "fatal flaws."

Let us look again at Tracy and Tracy (1998) to see how they framed the research problem. When we left the article, they had just usefully complicated the concept of emotion labor with two recent streams of conflicting findings. At this point, the authors explain that empathic concern—"a concern about the other's welfare without feeling the other's emotion"—has been found to be a modality between high and low involvement that reduces "burnout" among employees who engage in emotion labor. They end the discussion with this observation: "It would be valuable to know if avoiding both high and low levels of involvement (or detachment) is also regarded as the ideal stance in emergency call-taking work" (p. 394). The sentence makes a satisfying transition to the scene of their study and also leads directly to their set of research questions:

RQ1: What do the emotional experiences of 911 call-takers and citizens look like?

RQ2: What are the institution's emotion expression/feeling rules? Is there evidence that call-takers distinguish between the two kinds? How do call-takers perpetuate or transform expression/feeling rules?

RQ3: What are the communicative practices that 911 call-takers use to cope with feelings during and after the calls?

You can readily see that these questions are not framed as hypotheses (which are very rare in qualitative research), but as open-ended queries about the *what* and the *how* of subjective experience and communicative practice. Perhaps anyone with an interest in how emergency service workers cope with their jobs could have come up with one or more of these questions. There are, however, no short cuts in well-executed scholarship. Readers will understand *why* these questions are being asked, particularly with respect to their implications for communication praxis, by having been led expertly through a theoretical argument informed by the relevant sets of literature.

There are many ways to manage the framing of research problems in qualitative inquiry. Not all of them are phrased as questions, and frequently authors will state the problem in narrative form. Some authors even deliver the essence of the problem within the first page of the article, in which case the cultural analysis carries more of the theoretical argument than is typical (see Philipsen, 1975, for an example). Such variations of structure and style usually come after one has mastered the conventional form.

The third component of an article's opening section is the scene description. Normally what you want to convey is a view of the scene's organization, history, routines, and key social actors, and to capture the flavor of the quotidian life there. A good scene description furnishes your reader with a functional knowledge of the scene, particularly those details identifiable as salient to the research problem and the analysis. Tracy and Tracy's (1998) fieldwork took place at the Citywest Emergency Communications Center, a call center located in a western U.S. urban setting. In three paragraphs, the authors direct our gaze from Citywest's technical operations to the intimacy of the call-taker's cubicle: We first learn about the routing and volume of calls to Citywest's emergency and nonemergency numbers, then about the call-takers' formal work protocols, and finally of the call takers' social world, elastically bounded by the length of their phone cords and their on- and off-job relationships with fellow call-takers. This sequencing is appropriate to the authors' purposes, because it ends with allusions to the employee talk that punctuates the work routines and plays a part in several of the emotion-labor strategies encountered later in the analysis.

The scene description is contained in Tracy and Tracy's (1998) "Methods and Background" section. Other authors will move it forward, perhaps placing it in the article's introduction—a strategy that usually means the author considers the scene to be intrinsic to the research problem. Starting the article with a well-crafted story about the scene can also be a way to compel the readers' interest. In other articles, the scene description can be a long set piece, with the author's discussion of method and participant role embedded within it, and the interpretations flowing through and out of it (see Novek, 1995, for an example). A different design can be found in Rosen (1985), whose article length scene description incorporates an analysis of the social drama of a corporate ceremony.

These strategies give you a glimpse of the flexibility that qualitative authors enjoy in shaping their work. Here are some questions to ask as you think about a scene description strategy: Are the research problem and the scene inseparable, or do you regard your scene as simply one among many manifestations of the research problem—as in Tracy and Tracy's call center? Should the scene description be used to capture attention and interest, or merely to report basic information? Should the scene function as a stand-alone set piece, or should it be developed as an evolving narrative that enfolds the threads of the analysis?

❖ REPORTING METHODS
AND ANALYTIC PROCEDURE

Qualitative researchers should give an accounting of their design and methods, including the observational or interview protocols, data encoding techniques, analysis procedures, and the conditions under which the study was conducted. The nature of this obligation is to provide essential information about how your study was done and demonstrate why the findings should be regarded as trustworthy (even when they disconfirm your presuppositions).

Quantitative and qualitative researchers differ in critical ways in what they choose to report. Reporting in quantitative articles tends to emphasize aspects of the study that can be replicated, such as its instruments, measurement, sample, and the order in which treatments are applied or survey items presented. Ideally, all sources of unintended variation should be controlled, if not excluded from the study. Thus, considerable attention is devoted to the steps taken to reduce uncertainty, instability, or anomaly in the conduct of the study.

As a qualitative researcher, your role is hardly to control variation of any kind. It would be damaging to a field study, to say nothing of the integrity of the people, to try to control the range of "response" by members of the community. Your field role is to *experience differences* in communication practices as they arise in the setting you are studying. In writing about how you did this, you should discuss the scope of your involvement in the scene, the specific modes of participation and analysis you found most useful, and any steps you took to enhance your access to and understanding of the varied practices or discourses. How did you seek approval from the responsible "gatekeeping" party, and who "sponsored" your introductions to the membership? How many contact hours (or other time units) did you spend at the site(s)? How did you direct your observational activity over time? How did the members interpret your research credentials, your roles and allegiances? In a more reflexive vein, how did you manage your field persona? (See Wellman, 1994, for a splendid account of these work process matters.) A study based on interviews will report a different set of techniques, such as sample criteria, respondent selection, interview format and protocol, the topics or questions covered, and how you and your participants created a sense of rapport.

Data analysis reporting in journal articles can sometimes mystify readers. Some authors tell us that their themes "emerged" from a deep familiarity with the evidence. Others would appear to believe that a convincing presentation of findings is all that is needed to vouch for the quality of their procedures. However, most researchers do follow systematic rules for examining data, searching for patterns within or across cases, drawing inferences about communicative phenomena, and rejecting false interpretations. By articulating the basis of these decisions, you enable readers to understand how interpretations were derived from data.

Certain elements of analytic procedure are regularly found in well-reported qualitative articles. You will find reports of the *coding systems* used to manage and retrieve data, and develop thematic configurations and concept constructions. Many of those who use computer software packages mention the program and the options they used. Descriptions of the volume of text consulted, how the analyst read (and reread) data texts, and how previous interpretations were modified on the basis of subsequent readings can help us understand the inferential process (Spiggle, 1994). The analyst's toolkit also includes many evaluative procedures: *triangulations* of data by investigator, method or source; *negative case analysis*, in which searches for disconfirming instances lead to refinements of a proposition or hypothesis; *theoretical saturation*, which signals diminishing returns of fieldwork for further defining concepts; *member checks*, which use informant interviews to test and realign the researcher's factual and interpretative knowledge; and *audit trails*, which are third-party reviews of the decision-making process using the full corpus of materials that accreted during the entire study (Lincoln & Guba, 1985). Whether or not you submit your study to an audit, good procedural reporting depends on diligent data-storage and record-keeping habits during your time in the field.

Finally, qualitative researchers have the ability to shift (expand, narrow, refine) the focus and methods of investigation in accordance with changing events and their evolving sense of what is important to study. Telling readers about changes in your design and field strategies can enhance their understanding of the contingent nature of the accounts you have written. In doing this, you need not feel any "rigor envy" regarding the putative certainties of quantitative research. If the idea of a continually changing social reality is at the heart of how they view human experience, how can qualitative researchers do otherwise but embrace the protean character of their own field experience?

❖   PRESENTING DATA AND
     DEVELOPING INTERPRETATIONS

With your analysis finished, you are now ready to write interpretations of the research experience. Here again, you will encounter more choices of representation than is the norm for articles based on quantitative data. The standard practice in social science articles is to create a section called "findings" or "results," in which you succinctly report the results of each test or analysis and tell us whether the hypotheses were supported or not. Although it would be an exaggeration to say that the standard results section "writes itself," it is nevertheless true that the author merely needs to show the results of statistical operations with reference to the study's expectations. Not surprisingly, the results section is often the shortest part of a quantitative article.

In contrast, the presentation of discursive data is often the longest part of the qualitative article. It is no exaggeration to say that the significance of your article ultimately depends on your ability to represent a cultural world with authenticity, completeness, and subtlety, as well as to invoke the appropriate analytic frames (e.g., communicative rules, routines, ideology, myth, narrative, and so on) that will produce higher-level inferences. Because qualitative studies entail the personal involvement of the researcher at many levels, authorial voice can be a rhetorical consideration for rendering the field experience. The article may be written from other points of view than that of the neutral observer and may use different narrative techniques and devices.

All of these aspects need to be well orchestrated for the article to succeed in its purpose. This work of orchestration is made easier by the fact that there are some common ways of organizing data, interpretation, style, and voice. Let us begin with the basic components—exemplars, interpretation, and analytic synthesis—and see how they are used in an excerpt from the Tracy and Tracy (1998) study.

Exemplars are episodes of social action or discourse that have been shaped in such a way as to advance an argument or illustrate features of the scene. Unlike quantitative reports—where, for example, the mean and standard deviation can represent a whole set of data—there is no feasible way to refer readers directly to all of your field materials (observations, interviews, visual evidence, etc.). Usually, though, many incidents, statements, or conversations may be found to connect to a particular theme or concept. One can then edit these materials and design exemplars that act as vivid examples of what you want to convey about the cultural scene or the social actor. An exemplar can also show the specific manner by which an interpersonal strategy, a cultural code, or a normative rule (or a departure from the rule) is concretized in everyday life. Finally—and this is important to the credibility of your project—exemplars are ways of showing readers that *you were there*, that you heard, saw, and participated in the events of this study.

In the words of Spiggle (1994), *interpretation* refers "to assessing the intentions and inferences of those one is studying . . . making sense of experience and behavior, and seeing or understanding some phenomenon in its own terms, grasping its essence (e.g., interpreting a cultural form)" (p. 491). One kind of interpretation in qualitative reports involves the emic reconstruction of the viewpoint or experience of the cultural other. That is, the texts, discourses, and actions of the other are understood by witnessing and documenting their points of correspondence to the researcher's own experience. Researchers also create interpretations by seeking patterns in meaning across contexts, situations, and individuals, and by deciphering the cultural codes (e.g., sacred and profane) of rituals and texts (Spiggle, 1994, pp. 497–500). Nearly all journal articles include lengthy accounts of interpretation that construe the form, content, and meaning of the other's life world. These passages of cultural explication are grounded in and made persuasive by the use of carefully chosen and strategically placed exemplars. Without exemplars, your effort at interpretation will probably lack evidential sufficiency and narrative potency. Without a good interpretation, your exemplars are likely to be directionless.

Analytic synthesis is the moment when interpretations and exemplars join with analytic frames to inform, critique, or extend a theoretical argument. Instances of analytic synthesis enable you to link aspects of the depicted cultural life to the study's research problems, much in the way described by Golden-Biddle and Locke (1997):

> Theoretical points alternate with data to document and make concrete the conceptualization proposed by the researchers. The proposed theoretical frameworks depend on the data, and the organizations and actors they symbolize, to support and demonstrate the conceptualizations in "real life." Conversely, the data depend on the theory to give them relevant meaning.... The theoretical framework shapes readers' apprehension of the data, and the data provide the form for the theory. (p. 65).

However, two cautions should be mentioned with respect to the use of analytic synthesis. First, lengthy elaborations of a theoretical point can potentially interrupt the flow of your cultural interpretation. The point can be introduced and discussed briefly, but save your critical debates about theories and concepts for the introductory or concluding sections of the article. Second, you do not want to intermingle interpretation and theoretical discussion to the point that the boundaries between them become lost or compromised. Some authors avoid this problem by delaying the analytic synthesis: The cultural interpretation unfolds in full; then, in a concluding section, the author proposes the theories or concepts that arise from the analysis. In any case, any midpassage use of analytic synthesis should be selective and justified.

The following excerpt from Tracy and Tracy's (1998) study of emotion labor at an emergency call center displays the three components (noted in bold and enclosed in brackets), and how the authors positioned them in the text:

> We have described some of the positive and negative emotions that call-takers express in doing their job. However, some of the "feelings" found to be central to the call-taking role seem more of a jumble than a single emotion.

This jumbling is particularly apparent for the feeling we label *powerlessness* [**Analytic synthesis**]. Powerlessness seems to be a complex combination of guilt, anger, sadness, and stress. Because of the separation between call-taking and dispatching duties, the call-takers have little power over the outcome of the calls. . . . Call-takers . . . referred to powerlessness in regard to suicide calls [**Interpretation with exemplars**]. Tiffany said, "You can't help but blame yourself" when people end up hurting themselves. Other call-takers lament the fact that they rarely know if their advice to callers does any good. Call-taker Sue said that "you pray you say the right thing," especially during "rape in progress" calls. Others say that it "gnaws" at you to never find out the result of a call. Indeed, we found this personally distressing [**Exemplar**]. During the first author's observation with Erika, a female called in breathing very heavily and said that her husband just threw a chair at her. Erika was asking questions but the caller wasn't answering back—possibly because she was too scared to say anything or because her husband was watching her. We just kept hearing heavy breathing and Erika said that she would stay on the line with her until the police arrived. Suddenly the phone disconnected and when Erika called back, she got the answering machine. We never found out the outcome of the call. Erika wrote up the information, sent it to dispatch, commented on how she hated not knowing what happened, and answered the next call. (Fieldnotes). (pp. 399–400)

Several things are noteworthy about the design of this excerpt. Coming near the end of a section titled "Expressed Emotions of Call-Takers," the idea of powerlessness aptly synthesizes the prior discussion of positive and negative experiences, and foreshadows the interpretation of suicide calls as a salient case of powerlessness. The exemplars are intended to convey a sense of the reality of powerlessness. Appearing first are the brief quotations by named call-takers and the paraphrased sentiments of "other call-takers," both of which explore facets of the lived experience of suicide-call situations. Then, a much longer excerpt, edited from observer notes, tells a story of the actual way in which a call provokes powerlessness. The story of Erika's call does more than simply tell a story, however; it indicates, in the last line, how powerlessness is a spike of emotion encompassed by the routine of work. To sum up, Tracy and Tracy (1998) problematize what they heard and saw in the field by synthesizing a concept from different, albeit coherent, pieces of evidence. They then show us the theme in action by crafting exemplars that serve specific purposes.

There is no one right way to order exemplars, interpretations, and analytic synthesis. Your decisions hinge as much on what you want the reader to experience as on how you want to structure your arguments. Do you want to give your readers a palpable sense of what goes on in the scene you studied? If so, you may wish to begin with an exemplar that evokes the scene or the research problem—as Tracy and Tracy (1998) did in their article. Do you want to provide a comprehensive view of a setting before your readers learn how the social actors interpret their own experience? In her study of inner-city African American youth culture, Eleanor M. Novek (1995) starts the section "The High School as a Social Environment" with a historical and demographic overview of West Urbania High School and its recent decline—setting the stage for focused interpretations of the struggles that young people face at school and in the community.

Similarly, the axiom "form follows function" applies to decisions about how to configure your data presentation. Qualitative studies do not always label their "findings" or "results" as such, and may actually take several sections to achieve their goals. Tracy and Tracy's (1998) study is an example of the conventional thematic form. Their data presentation takes place in one long section, "The Case Study," within which several subsections explicate the emotional side of emergency call-takers' communication: first, the range of emotional experience; second, the institutional feeling rules; third, the emotion-labor strategies the callers employ (arguably the heart of their analysis). Other studies, such as Novek's (1995) ethnography, develop narratives of cultural life. The main sections of her study are overlapping views of the community, defined mostly by the students' attitudes: "West Urbania as Home," "The High School as a Social Environment," "Inner-City Youth Culture: Uncool in School," and "Resistance and Reframing." Studies using a multisite or multiperson case study approach often organize the presentation by persons, groups, or organizations. Lichterman's (1992) study sought to peer inside the interpretive practices of self-help book readers and how the reading informs their sense of self. After articulating conclusions based on exemplars from the entire sample of fifteen interviewees, his interpretation focused on case studies of three readers who relate to popular psychology books in strikingly different ways. The major rule to take away from this discussion is that an article's organization should flow out of the logic that the author developed for explaining the field evidence.

Authorial voice is another challenge for presenting data and developing interpretations—indeed, for writing the research article *in toto*. *Voice* refers to the modes of expression that the author uses to influence how readers understand the text. Among the chief considerations of voice in qualitative research are the following: (a) the relation of author to the reader; (b) the relation of author to the human subjects in the field; (c) the author's inscribed temporal and social presence in the scene; (d) the manipulation of action, words, and scene to achieve reader effects; and (e) stylistic aspects that construct the author's persona. All of these aspects of voice affect the claims of the article and the reader's attitude toward them.

If we look back at the Tracy and Tracy (1998) excerpt, several features of their (collective) voice are apparent. For the most part, the authors' interpretive control over the subjects' voices and what their experiences mean is rather strong. Although the authors refer to themselves as "we" (except when attention shifts to "the first author"), they interpret the callers' discourse through a rhetoric of objective knowledge. However, when we come to Erika's story, the narrative shifts to a more subjective view of the action. The "we" now becomes the author and Erika, forcing the reader to identify more closely with the participants in this event. The line, "Indeed, we found this distressing," is a very interesting moment because, for most of the article, Tracy and Tracy describe the emotional predicaments of their subjects at a rather detached pitch.

Although there is not an opportunity here to explore this important topic, you should at least know that you already have an authorial voice, however "untrained" it may be. Whether your voice helps or hinders your ability to achieve desired effects in your research writing is another matter. If at some point you wish to engage in qualitative research at a professional level, you would do well to read the literature on ethnographic voice, authorship, and the politics of the researcher and the researched—particularly writings that challenge or extend the conventional practice of writing (see, for example, Clifford & Marcus, 1986; Mitchell & Charmaz, 1996; Taylor, 1997).

❖ CONCLUSION

What difference do qualitative studies make, not only in the academy, but also in the public sphere and the everyday lives of people? In what sense are they worth the enormous effort put into them, to say nothing of the trust that the social actors often place in the researcher?

Answering these questions is one more challenge of writing qualitative research—perhaps the most important challenge. Most of us who do this kind of work—and even those who simply read and evaluate it—often face these questions. In my view, qualitative research addresses enduring needs for knowing how culture is reproduced, how value and power are constituted, how people experience their selves in relation to the larger cultural order, and how communication across cultural identities and systems can be accomplished. Out of these broad needs come many of the specific problems studied by communication scholars, such as (mis)conceptions about the other's competence or morality, the situations of the dispossessed and the disenfranchised, and the ways in which power and resistance are actually performed. Scholars are one of the few groups in society that can engage these problems with only the public as the beneficiary of their work.

However, as both apologist and critic of qualitative communication research, I continue to want more from the research that we do. Each project of communication research changes the world it seeks to study. Yet we seldom think very carefully about what these interventions really mean. We seldom think about how insular the audiences for the vast bulk of our work really are. We don't often consider how our experiences from the field *could* come into contact with experiences of the larger world. Of course, the written products of our research lie squarely at the intersection of these issues. Among the challenges for the future will be to expand the formats and outlets in which we write at the same time that we try to understand how our work can make a social and ethical difference.

❖ REFERENCES

Anderson, J. A. (1996). *Communication theory: Epistemological foundations.* New York: Guilford.

Carbaugh, D., & Hastings, S. O. (1992). A role for communication theory in ethnography and cultural analysis. *Communication Theory, 2,* 156–164.

Clifford, J., & Marcus, G. E. (Eds.). (1986). *Writing culture: The poetics and politics of ethnography.* Berkeley, CA: University of California Press.

Geertz, C. (1973). Thick description: Toward an interpretive theory of culture. In *The interpretation of cultures* (pp. 3–30). New York: Basic Books.

Golden-Biddle, K., & Locke, K. D. (1997). *Composing qualitative research.* Thousand Oaks, CA: Sage.

Eisenhardt, K. M. (1989). Building theories from case study research. *Academy of Management Review, 14,* 532–550.

Lichterman, P. (1992). Self-help reading as a thin culture. *Media, Culture and Society, 14,* 421–447.

Lincoln, Y. S., & Guba, E. G. (1985). *Naturalistic inquiry.* Beverly Hills, CA: Sage.

Lindlof, T. R., & Taylor, B. C. (Forthcoming). *Qualitative communication research methods* (2nd ed.). Thousand Oaks, CA: Sage.

Mitchell, R. G., Jr., & Charmaz, K. (1996). Telling tales, writing stories: Postmodernist visions and realist images in ethnographic writing. *Journal of Contemporary Ethnography, 25,* 144–166.

Morris, M. (1998). Publishing perils, and how to survive them: A guide for graduate students. *Cultural Studies, 12,* 498–512.

Novek, E. M. (1995). West Urbania: An ethnographic study of communication practices in inner-city youth culture. *Communication Studies, 46,* 169–186.

Philipsen, G. (1975). Speaking "like a man" in Teamsterville: Culture patterns of role enactment in an urban neighborhood. *Quarterly Journal of Speech, 61,* 13–22.

Potter, W. J. (1996). *An analysis of thinking and research about qualitative methods.* Hillsdale, NJ: Lawrence Erlbaum.

Rosen, M. (1985). Breakfast at Spiro's: Dramaturgy and dominance. *Journal of Management, 11,* 31–48.

Spiggle, S. (1994). Analysis and interpretation of qualitative data in consumer research. *Journal of Consumer Research, 21,* 491–503.

Taylor, B. C. (1997). Home zero: Images of home and field in nuclear-critical studies. *Western Journal of Communication, 61,* 209–234.

Tracy, S. J., & Tracy, K. (1998). Emotion labor at 911: A case study and theoretical critique. *Journal of Applied Communication Research, 26,* 390–411.

Vidich, A. J., & Lyman, S. M. (1994). Qualitative methods: Their history in sociology and anthropology. In N. K. Denzin & Y. S. Lincoln (Eds.), *Handbook of qualitative research* (pp. 23–59). Thousand Oaks, CA: Sage.

Wellman, D. (1994). Constituting ethnographic authority: The work process of field research. *Cultural Studies, 8,* 569–583.

Wolcott, H. F. (1990). *Writing up qualitative research.* Newbury Park, CA: Sage.

7

The Challenge of
Writing the Interpretive Inquiry

James A. Anderson

❖ ❖ ❖

Interpretive inquiry is a vigorous and rowdy species that seeks to manage it own excesses and contradictions by continually reinventing itself, rather than fixing on a particular set of writing conventions. Denzin (1997) has traced six different movements (including the unreadable present) during this century, with the majority occurring in the last 20 years. He notes,

> Each of the earlier historical moments is still operating in the present, either as legacy or as a set of practices that researchers still follow or argue against. . . . Multiple criteria of evaluation now compete for attention in this field. There have never been so many paradigms, strategies of inquiry, or methods of analysis to draw on. We are in a moment of discovery and rediscovery as new ways of looking, interpreting, arguing, and writing are debated and discussed. (p. 19)

Even discounting a very human trait to consider its own era as uniquely superior or desperate, this does seem like a particularly difficult moment to be giving advice on how to write this stuff. It seems as though nearly anything can be published and nearly everything will be rejected somewhere. This chapter, therefore, deals with one particular form of qualitative inquiry—empirical hermeneutics (Anderson, 1996).

Qualitative research of this sort starts when the researcher intentionally enters into an authentic experience, seeks to achieve the level of member knowledge needed to interpret that experience as a member would, and then deliberately engages both the experience and the knowledge upon which it depends as objects of study.

The field-work phase of this research privileges presence—the direct experience of what it means to "be there"—but the activity that makes being there research is writing. From the simplest site notes to field notes to episodes to the most complex ethnographic argument, writing is the distinctive craft of the ethnographer. At any of these levels, such writing always begins with "the facts of the case" that demonstrate the presentness of the ethnographer and authenticate the interpretation that is the heart of the matter. It is the interpretation, however, that makes the contribution to our knowledge (Anderson, 1987).

For the empirical hermeneutics scholar the writing task is to take what appears to be in its factual presentation and to reconstitute it for what it is in its significance. In Atkinson's (1990) words, "The ethnographer constructs versions of social reality, and persuades his or her reader of the authenticity, plausibility and significance of the representations of social scenes or settings" (p. 57).

In this writing, there is invention everywhere—in the events, in the facts, in the author's claims, and in the reader's interpretation.[1] As Van Maanan (1988) has put it, we tell tales. The truth of our tale is in the strength—the resonance—of the narrative that produces it. Empirical hermeneutics writing is a narrative structure the purpose of which is to drive home a particular interpretive claim. The claim appears in that moment when the analyst's experience "makes sense." It is at that point that the tale can be told.

For me, that point occurs long after I have left the field. It happens as I sit with my notes and artifacts trying to write the episodes of the action —those descriptive stories that achieve *vraisemblance,* that compelling resonance—as they meet the requirements of the narrative and capture the meaningful qualities of the action.[2] Episodes are not the final argument—

the journal article, chapter, or book—that constitutes the ethnographic claims, but they are its foundation. Much of the final writing in the ethnography that I read either centers on the episodes and interweaves an exegesis, or centers on an interpretation and interweaves exemplars from episodes. In this chapter, I will provide you with advice on writing the former: a narrative episode interwoven with analysis directed toward a contribution to theory.

The last bit of advice in this introduction is that ethnography is a life's work, not a research form or a writing style (Rose, 1990). I suppose there are those far more clever than I who can pick this work up on a moment's notice, but for me the work is the everyday experience of participating, observing, reflecting, and writing. Far and away, my model for this life is the work of Dwight Conquergood (1991). Excellence can also be found in the work of Mara Adelman and Larry Frey (1996), and in the more theoretical efforts of John Shotter (1993) and Kenneth Gergen (1997), among many others. A fistful of examples can be found in the May and November, 1995, special issues of *Communication Studies* (e.g., Procter, 1995) and of *Communication Theory* (e.g., Nicotera, 1999), but do not neglect the work of Nick Trujillo (*Communication Studies 292*, 1997), Lyle Crawford (1996), or Eric Eisenberg (Eisenberg, 1990) either.

For the rest of this chapter, I would like to demonstrate this life of writing by centering on an episode from my wilderness studies,[3] then probing it with exemplars of the analytical claims that I might make. What I want to show is how the narrative structure opens entry points for analysis and how theory makes that analysis both sensible and worthwhile.

Our writing task begins with the narrative of the episode itself. Writing that narrative is not ingenuous; it is a planned effort, because no event speaks for itself. The narrative has two responsibilities: first, to demonstrate the authenticity of the observation, and second, to achieve sufficient complexity to allow the analysis to make its contribution to understanding.

The authenticity of observation is documented when the writing demonstrates that the researcher is (a) inside the action, (b) somehow a stakeholder in it, and (c) methodically recording its process. The episode I present here is of the autoethnographic sort, in that there is mostly a single voice represented.[4] That single voice, the nature of the wilderness experience, and the fact that it was a father/daughter episode allow me to use a modified "Hero's Tale" format in the telling. My choice of the hero's tale intends to capture the reader and put her or him in the action, accomplishing the first two of our three responsibilities. (It grants me other liberties and imposes responsibilities as well, which I will point out as we go along.)

To reach the third element—the methodic record—autoethnographic episodes of the ordinary (I do not do "exotics") have an intensified dependence on detail to authenticate the attentiveness of the author. However, it is not detail for its own sake: The detail must make sense of the action, must support and move the narrative. You can judge my success for yourself in these opening paragraphs, after which we will return to the responsibility of analysis.

AN EPISODE

The only animals that I have watched drown were the big Norway rats that used to inhabit the sheep shed. Because sheep eat poison and are caught in spring traps, the rats had to be captured in a live trap—the *Hava-Heart*—a device marketed as a humane, "catch and release" method. In this case, the trap, rats and all, was thrown into a barrel of water and held down with a rock until the rats died. The myth of the rat is that they are fierce survivors. The evidence in watching these animals die supports that myth. Each animal would work for several minutes trying to escape. I often thought about the length of time it took to drown a rat—so much longer than I could hold my breath underwater.

My daughter and I are running the riffles and rapids of the lower San Juan. I have done this stretch before with her younger sister. As on that trip, Dave and his wife Susan are in the second canoe and their son Gavin is piloting the supply raft. My canoeing experience dates back nearly 40 years, but little of it has been in rated white water. This stretch of the San Juan has only one rated run—Government Rapids—which gets a 2.5 on a scale of 10. Destination canoeists have little reason to run rapids. There is always a way around them. The point for those who do run them is the stage that the water provides to play a scene. The scene here was a moderate version of the *Thrill Seekers*. There is both evidence for and mystic aspect to the danger of the river. The current is swift; the canyon walls can prevent escape for hundred of yards. The rocks are harder than a human head, and, launched into the stream, the human body becomes a projectile that can be hurled into those rocks by the current with great force. But our knowledge of the danger is established more by Park Service rules and actor tales than by actual experience. By rule, canoeists must have life jackets, extra paddles, and supplies to repair rock-torn holes in both bodies and canoes. The actors tell stories of past dumpings and of deaths they have heard about. We all do a lot of rehearsing: what will happen; what to do in the event of a disaster. The inevitability of a disaster is contained in the motto that there are two kinds of river runners—those who have flipped and those who will.

At this level, running rapids is barely technical. By Park Service permits, the river has been predetermined as within the competency of nearly everyone—any rapids too frightening can be walked around. If you get into trouble, it is because you asked for it. The river itself presents a fairly reliable map for the routes through its trouble spots. You can spot the shoals and rocks with good certainty. It is the wind and pressure waves that are unpredictable.

My daughter and I spend the first day nearly uneventfully. We had one unexpected 180 at the end of a run when an eddy spun us around. Other than my embarrassment for this lapse at the stern, no rock was struck, no damage done. Even without this event, there has been great fun: Hearing my daughter's exclamation as we hit the first set of pressure waves, which lift the front of the canoe four feet out of the water and slam it back down on the next rise, is as much a rush for me as for her. These pressure waves run in straight stacks; by keeping the canoe perpendicular to the set, there is a great ride to be had. The water from the waves pours over the bow position and would swamp an open canoe. Our canoe is, of course, skirted—covered by canvas which keeps the waves out and the gear in.

The structure of this narrative, as noted, is a modified hero's tale in which the narrator will be tested by the events (see, for examples, Campbell, 1968; Daly, 1973). The test and its interpretation are set up in the drowning rat introduction. In some way or another, we expect the mystery of the introduction to be solved by the narrative's conclusion and to learn something about the character of the narrator. There is much richness in the river, its management, and the narrator's experience on it. We should not be surprised at this, as the narrative writing is intended to evoke this richness in order to establish the character of the analytic contribution I can make.

Notice the two-step relationship here: First, the experience creates the foundation for the narrative. But there are several other narratives that could be drawn from that experience; narrative rarely exhausts experience. On the other hand, my experience is simply private knowledge; it is the narrative—the second step—that moves experience into the public sphere and creates the terms of our contribution.

The choice of narrative form is driven by analytical goals, because the narrative creates the resource for the analysis. The analysis cannot reach beyond those resources and still maintain its empirical character. Though unwarranted criticism can run forever, critical analysis can readily exhaust a weak narrative. My choice of the hero's tale allows me to comment on the character of the modern wilderness and its latter-day heroes. It also forces me to constitute a quest, danger, setbacks, and some resolution. The events provide the resources for those narrative elements, but forces none of them. On the other hand, a different set of events might provide inadequate resources, and the narrative would fail for lack of *vraisemblance*.

We turn now to the responsibility of analysis. Analytical writing of this sort requires three different types of knowledge, all of about equal import. First, the analyst has to have a thorough knowledge of the local performance—the action of the narrative. This knowledge is built out of the participant-observation activities of the research study. Second, the analyst must have a deep knowledge of the cultural themes that are in play. In the analysis of this episode, for example, we would need to know the beliefs and values of the Native Americans and ranchers who hold the river as heritage, the texts and regulations of the federal managers, and the tracts and broadsides of conservation groups, developers, and miners. We would need to know of the bitter fights between federal managers and the San Juan County Commission, and between some conservation groups and everyone else. We would have to understand the differences of river performance within the standards of kayakers, canoeists, rafters, fishers, locals, and tourists, among others. Third, the analyst must have a knowledge of the interpretive theory that she or he is going to put into play.

The narrative presents a number of interpretive routes at this juncture. For my part, I am a social action theorist concerned with the semiotic character of action (Anderson, 1996). I would use theory to break into this performance to illuminate the "rules of significance" by which the meaningfulness of what is done is created. Others might use narratology to explicate the hero's-tale structure that this episode takes (something we do here at a very elementary level). Still others might make use of feminist ecology theory to approach this masculine performance. Any number of other theoretical standpoints could be taken, but some theory needs to be present both to support the analysis and to be the location of the contribution of the analysis.

This year the river is low—running at 1900 cubic feet per second. Western rivers are basically watering troughs for western cities. River flows are determined by release schedules at the various impoundments. The lower flow means the pressure waves are much less a force to reckon with, but the current seems faster. Dave and I get into a discussion over what determines current speed. The gradient of the bed or the volume of water, or both. I spend a good number of strokes devising an experiment to find out; images of a PBS program on 17th-century science flash into the design.

The winds nearly always rise in the afternoon. The canyon walls send them racing up the river, stalling the canoes and reversing rafts. The fuzzy romance of drifting is gone. Progress now is work. The bow and stern positions do different kinds of work. The canoeist in the bow can do little to control the direction of the canoe. His or her job is to provide steady power—steerage, it's called—by continuous repetitions of the straight stroke: The paddle is held by its throat and top handle and drawn straight back. The directional influences that the bow can exert are through the bow rudder, the backstroke (back paddle), and the very useful rock-and-bank push. The last is strictly a pragmatic move, but even it has style with the practical outcome of avoiding damage to the paddle edge. The person in the stern both controls and provides the primary power for the canoe. Because of the fluid dynamics of the classic canoe design, each stroke from the stern can easily overpower the opposing torque from the bow stroke. If both canoeists do the straight stroke, the canoe begins to inscribe a large circle away from the stern paddle. Consequently the primary stern stroke is the J-stroke—a straight stroke with a correcting rudder at the end. The stern position controls the direction of the canoe through the sweep stroke, the rudder, back rudder, and back paddle. Canoeists do not alternate sides, but switch only for tactical reasons or out of fatigue. Switching sides is a statement about your skill, your personal fitness, or the conditions of the river.

The second day has the major runs for the trip. We stop to scout the first rapids of some reputation. Scouting is a contested practice. It is recommended by the books, and we nearly always do it for the big runs. My daughter claims that it serves to *epicize* the action. (I do not ask then, but later find out that this is a technical term out of her clinical work.) It is certainly true that the river at canoe level looks little like the river from the bank. The height and force of the pressure waves have to be felt and ridden on to know their effect. Nevertheless, scouting does reveal likely entrances and generally shows the routes through the run.

This scouting read turns out to be deceptive, directing attention to false dangers and minimizing the force of the waves. Our troubles start even before we begin the shoot. We have landed too close to the run in stopping to scout. When we got back on the river, the action is upon us before I can completely secure the seat curtain around my waist to close off the access hole in the skirt. I have to give up pulling on the elastics to put the canoe on the tongue. For the moment, I am losing it. I try a stroke, pull on the elastics; the canoe doesn't respond, pulled by the current or wind. I miss a stroke. "Come on, damn it, do it!" I rudder us onto the route, but slightly too close to the canyon wall. We are riding off square to the waves. Water pours into the stern. The canoe angles toward the wall. "No, damn it!" Three hard sweep strokes; the canoe slides by, and the river turns flat. Sponging out the last of the water as we float along, I know I should have ruddered on the opposite side. The canoe would have responded much faster. It is a common failing in my technique: I would rather work than wait.

The opening sentence of this section establishes the foundation for a theme park interpretation of the wilderness (remember, my intent is the analysis of wilderness; the narrative is my vehicle). What makes the wilderness wild is in the hands of human controllers. The extension of this thematic analysis could come from interviews with the "dam operators," locals, tour guides, tourists, and the other members of the trip; stories in the state's newspapers; and guide books, tourist information pamphlets, and other such texts. The purpose of this analysis would be to discover the frontstage/backstage thematic differences between those who play on the river and those who work on the river. (I am relatively secure in my theme park interpretation given that land managers describe themselves as retailers who provide "customer service" in "one-stop shopping" for all one's primitive experience needs.)

The long paragraph on canoeing strokes has a two-fold authenticating purpose. First, the ethnographer has a responsibility to tell the story in the codes of the members. Vocabularies and discursive forms make a difference in our understanding of the action. The second purpose is to establish the authority of the narrator as a competent performer in this theatre of action. (It had better be right, or it will have the opposite effect.) If the analyst cannot manage the language, it is unlikely that she or he can manage the action. This member authority is needed to maintain the narrative in its proper empirical context.

The action of the narrative is the first test of the protagonist in this mini-heroic form. The narrator succeeds, he tells us, in somewhat less than elegant style. Chastened, he attempts to learn from his mistakes and recognizes a long-standing failing. He does not question the wisdom of his being there, nor can he for it to remain a simple hero's tale.

That combination gives us an additional insight into the wilderness experience. I might argue that the wilderness is a managed stage in which we can perform "the test" of the heroic form. I would need to develop the theory of " the test" and of the "heroic form." I would need to show how the management processes of permits, controlled entry, water releases, and the like produce the stage of "wilderness" out of an area that is merely sparsely populated.

The episode provides the justification for that claim, but it does not do any of that work. That work is the third kind of writing required, where the analyst makes the connection of her or his experience to an existing body of interpretive theory.

There is, of course, a major transition to be managed as we take the all too familiar into the all too arcane. For my critical eye, the biggest danger in that transition is that the preexisting formulas of the theory simply take over the writing and the experience disappears. Again, from this reader's perspective, a good deal of continental and British sociology (e.g., Baudrillard, de Certeau, Hall, Giddens), although brilliant theory, fails to maintain its connection to experience.

Time and again we need to go back to the story for extended visits. If our writing only uses theory to explain experience (the sort of writing where experience appears only on wholly opportunistic occasions), we have accomplished only half the task. Experience has to penetrate theory, make its contribution to theory. It has to survive the encounter.[5]

The entrance to Government Rapids looks nothing like the last time we were here. Only the sound alerts me to the significance of this rapids. We turn around and head back up river to avoid our last mistake. As we put in to shore, Dave catches up in the second canoe and Gavin comes on in the raft. Dave, Gavin, and I go scouting. Angela decides she doesn't want to look; she just wants to do it.

The rapids has a big drop in the middle. The last time I ran it, the route was to the right. This time the right is completely guarded by rocks and appears to be quite shallow. We will have to take the drop in the middle. Dave grumbles about the dam keepers and why the river is so low. The entrance to the tongue—that convex of water that marks the clear path through the obstacles—is a difficult S. One must avoid rocks on the left, and thread the canoe between two mounders where the tongue flows. The tongue is narrow and the boulders that the water mounds over create pressure waves from the left and the right. The only chance we have is to lay it on the tongue and hope to get by. Dave hesitates. I decide there is nothing more to learn, and tell Angela it's a toss up, but a piece of cake.

This time, we are far enough up stream to get completely ready. The wind picks up as we start out. Wouldn't you know it? The rocks on the left come up quick. I beat the wind; I am in control, ruddering perfectly through the S. The tongue is much narrower than I scouted. It's also very convex. I watch the water fall away from the sides of the canoe as we enter the drop. The drop is steep. The wind or a current pushes us left. The pressure wave from that boulder slugs the side of the canoe pitching us to the gunnels. We both oppose, pulling the canoe back. In the rebound, the wave catches us again and we are flipped.

I am trapped under the canoe, my right leg wedged under the seat and held in place by the skirt. I tell myself that I'm okay. I crawl up the side of the canoe and push my head just above the water to catch a breath. As I go back under to work on my leg, I slam into a boulder. The phrase "I don't think I'm going to like this" drifts into my mind. The rehearsed dangers of being knocked out and dying unnoticed beneath the canoe become present. My conscious self is notably calm. When does the panic of drowning come? I crawl up again and can't quite get my face out of the water. I literally purse my lips to catch air. I can't breathe in. My lungs are still full. I am back under the canoe for the third, maybe the last, time, but my leg releases. I shoot up to the surface no longer resigned, but in charge. I luxuriate in a moment of breathing. It's a nice feeling.

Angela is riding with one hand on the keel. She had kicked free immediately, came up away from the canoe, and swam back to it. She could not find me and was figuring a rescue. Now, we're all business. Canoes do not sink. With the tail of the rapids rushing around us, we roll the canoe back over. I climb in; she grabs her paddle as it floats by. I grab the spare still tucked in the skirt, and we see the stern paddle just ahead of us. I tell Angela to get in and go for it. She says something I don't understand, but finally gets around to getting the job done. Later, on shore, she remarked that she went into shock at that moment because she knew we were safe.

We bail the canoe, drain the camp box, check the food, and hope the dry bags have done their job. Angela and I sit on the bank and begin the re-counting. We tell each other our own stories, and work out an understanding of what happened. I am relieved when she says that she is happy that she has this memory. I reach up and adjust my hat. A simple baseball cap, it is still on my head; my glasses, which were carefully tied on and secured to my shirt, are gone.

The next and last rapids of this trip is Slick Horn. It is probably the third most difficult on the river. We hike the canyon first for a diversion, but we know we have to run the rapids. Angela is understandably worried. She is inexperienced, and I am of diminished visual capacity at 20/250. I tell her not to worry, that it's just like "Mr. Magoo Goes Canoeing." She is amused but not amused. Dave says, "Good luck," in more of a comment than a wish. We make it easily, but with a war whoop from me that is entirely inappropriate for the difficulty. I can hear the rafters parked downstream sniff their disdain (but anybody can ride a marshmallow in this river).

In this section, the hero's tale takes us through the test and to the transitional boundary where the narrator has to reenter the community to share his experience with the members. In the hero tale, the test has not been successfully passed unless the community learns from it and changes the conditions that required it.

We will learn of that response in the next section. At this point, the success of the story lies in the convincing evidence that at least one form of the wilderness experience matches the metanarrative of the hero's tale. A minor insight, to be sure, but we can then take advantage of the now-receptive reader to explore, say, the controversies of wilderness politics. For example, how the West—and particularly Utah—is being carved up for tourist heroes, or how wilderness regulations of "leave no trace" can be reinterpreted as efforts to manage the fantasy stage. These are provocative, even contentious, interpretations that are now given standing by the success of the narrative.

I am now watching and participating in the construction of this experience. I recall the line I thought while under the water. It is a line from a story Tom Walker told me about the time he "crashed and burned" during a ski race. He thought it while waiting for his descent from an inadvertent launching. Even my most critical moments are intertextual. Dave, who walked Government Rapids that day, has told me what I did wrong when the canoe hit the rock. We never hit the rock. Is this Western accountability or selective memory? What about karma as an explanation? I have remembered the rats. Will I remember the leg the next time I canoe? Has this been deep play? What was I to learn? I felt no nervousness on the river, but now my hands shake as I type. Is this writing romantic hermeneutics? Why don't I know what has happened to me in this happening? The event may actually have been trivial. There may have been no real danger, but my right leg has a double bruise, one on the thigh and another on the calf. The calf was under the seat. The thigh pressed up against the gunnel as I reached for air. The seat is bent where I rolled the 16-gauge hardened aluminum with the force of my effort. I have not been able to bend it back. My mind was calm, ready to accept my imagined fate; my body clearly said no.

The story would have come out anyway, not that we really wanted to contain it. Angela has her own reasons for the telling. For me, people knew I had gone; it's hard to disguise a limp. The story will be told by Dave for his own understanding of the river, but more important, it is a wonderful opportunity to enact self and other. The response to the story has been mixed.

Some empathize; others yawn, of course. I have been asked about my wife's response; told I was irresponsible or at least unthinking of my familial duties as well as those of the office; accused of being macho; scolded in both loving and reproachful ways and told not to do it again; and bonded in thanks for my survival. Nobody has asked me if I had fun. I did.

It has been widely reported that a heavy burden of Vietnam veterans was the failure of the community to complete the veterans' story. They answered the call, met the test, but when they returned, they were shunned; their voice unheard. We have to find ourselves in the mirror of the other. The narrator relays to us his own confusion as to how to understand his experience. He takes his tale to the community for confirmation, only to hear the same babble of voices as in his head. The community's response seems to turn on the quality of the quest. Those who reject the message—the message of every hero's tale concerns a communal failure—reject the narrator's quest as an appropriate vehicle of change. "Boys and girls playing John Wesley Powell on the river just don't make it." The narrator nonetheless marvels in his own change and the joy he found in it.

The final turn of this tale is to craft the linkages back to the social performances that create it. At this point, my advice takes its most controversial turn. Most scientific writing is based on the premise of Hume's gap—David Hume's argument that only what is true is under scientific scrutiny whereas what is good is beyond its reach. We can, according to Hume, declare "what is" but not "what ought to be." Postmodernism's reduction of science from the divine (Latour, 1987; Prelli, 1989; Rorty, 1979) has demonstrated that science's claim of "what is" is equally a claim of "what ought to be" and has advanced the claim that Hume's gap is actually an artificial separation from responsibility.

The result of closing Hume's gap is to open the necessity of speaking the truths of what good our work entails. This particular episode allows us to focus on the management of life-threatening risks in the performance of a life worth living. What appears to be interesting is the criticism the narrator received from those who felt him foolish and his persistence in feeling good about the experience. (To be sure, that criticism would have to be presented in much more detail in the narrative to allow this analysis.) I can see a claim developing that such risk taking is a necessary action for men and women in order to justify their own subject position within a late-capitalist culture. The claim "I have deliberately faced death," however minimally true, is a cultural separator.

Not all editorial gatekeepers will allow this writing. A writer always needs to find the proper venue for the work. Read the publications of the journal or publishing house that you might consider for submission. Pay attention to changes in editorial leadership and direction. Simplistic advice, perhaps, but I am still getting manuscripts for a journal I edited three years ago. Let me end with a segment from Part II of my wilderness studies. If I have advised you well, you should recognize the different structure of this narrative, begin immediately to note the entry points of analysis, and consider the potential standpoints of theory that would house its contribution. Capture this vision and the writing will follow.

PART II

The carry-boat is giving us a great ride across the length of Moose Lake. The Moose is a challenging lake for canoeists. Nearly 5 miles long, it dangles at the entrance of the Boundary Waters canoe area like a thigh and drumstick. The wind blows east to west down its full length in the morning, and west to east up its full length in the evening. Angela and I are headed east in the traditional morning start, which makes the economics of the carry boat work, to retrace a trip I took at the end of my youth. We have 75 miles of lakes and portages planned. The route takes us up the Man chain (That Man, No Man, This Man, and Man lakes) to the gaping western bay of Saganagons Lake. This area has been fully glaciated in each of the ice ages. The result is a predominance of granite in cliffs, boulders, and sharp rocks, the last of which lurk just below the surface of the veneer of pine needles that deceptively invites your sleeping bag.

The lakes are the gouges of the glaciers with boundaries of deposits or unyielding terrain. Though the acts of creation came from a single system, the results vary widely. Some lakes are fathomless, hypothermic, and populated by lake trout, the trophies of the region. Others reflect the entropic action of generations of pine deaths, and have mellowed into soft-bottomed havens of crawfish and the prized bass. In the in-between are walleyes (the other prized fish), northerns, the occasional muskie, and all the feeder fish—rock bass, bluegills, sunfish, and perch.

In my twelfth year, I came alone by train, bus, and a daredevil ride in a milk truck to spend a month camping and canoeing. In the late 50s, I brought various urban friends up here to introduce them to the manly life. It *was* manly then, and there is no nostalgia in the change. The last of these trips ended in a great fight, which splintered the nucleus and finished the series. I returned in the late 60s for a couple of trips on the American side. The 1967 Arab-Israeli war was fought in its entirety during one of them. Now, 23 years later, I am back.

I am uncertain as to why my daughter is with me. I invited her and she accepted is the simple tale, but that's never the story. We work a relationship that is intimate and distant, warm and calculating at the same time. The intellect dominates the heart in equal measure. But she is here in her twenty-sixth year, between partners, on furlough from her job, to spend two weeks with her dad and whatever else she intends. I could tell about the drive out—the haggling over whose turn it was to drive (the very question that broke up that old gang of mine), the feint of a collision with a concrete bridge, the speeding ticket, the reckless changing of drivers at 70 miles per hour—but the journey is not the lesson.

Instead, we are on the boat speeding our way to Canadian customs and our first portage. I begin here to capture the moment of the end.

❖ NOTES

1. Proponents of the strong program hold this widespread invention to be true of objective writing also. For them, objective writing simply masks its invention through its own conventions of writing and ignores the reader altogether. It is truth through deception.

2. Note the presumption here: that action has a preexisting unity and coherence into which actors improvisationally play. The analyst's interpretation reveals this unity and coherence. This interpretive route is simply denied by many other theoretical standpoints. Most forms of cognitivism, with their insistence on methodological individualism, could not approach the preexistence of the coherence of action, seeing that coherence as a metaconstruction by the analyst out of the individual acts produced.

3. My so-called wilderness studies are attempts to understand the cultural standing of wilderness within my participation in the action that is centered there. That participation started with boyhood scouting experiences and includes experiences in Europe, New Zealand, and Australia; my episodic writing about it started about 20 years ago. The events of this episode happened 11 years ago.

4. All single-authored works (and many co-authored works) are single voiced. No amount of quotation of the "other" can offset the control the author has of the writing situation. Unless the other can also become the author, single-voiced works are always autoethnographic.

5. It rarely does in cultural studies, surveys, and experiments.

❖ REFERENCES

Adelman, M., & Frey, L. (1996). *The fragile community: Living together with AIDS.* Mahwah, NJ: Lawrence Erlbaum.

Anderson, J. A. (1987). *Communication research: Issues and methods.* New York: McGraw-Hill.

Anderson, J. A. (1996). *Communication theory: Epistemological foundations.* New York: Guilford.

Atkinson, P. (1990). *The ethnographic imagination: Textual constructions of reality.* London: Routledge.

Campbell, J. (1968). *The hero with a thousand faces* (2nd ed.). Princeton, NJ: Bollinger.

Communication Studies 292. (1997). Fragments of the self at the postmodern bar. *Journal of Contemporary Ethnography, 26,* 251–292.

Conquergood, D. (1991). Rethinking ethnography: Toward a cultural politics. *Communication Monographs, 58,* 179–194.

Crawford, L. (1996). Personal ethnography. *Communication Monographs, 63,* 158–170.

Daly, M. (1973). *Beyond God the father: Toward a philosophy of women's liberation.* Boston: Beacon.

Denzin, N. K. (1997). *Interpretive ethnography: Ethnographic practices for the 21st century.* Thousand Oaks, CA: Sage.

Eisenberg, E. (1990). Jamming: Transcendence through organizing. *Communication Research, 17,* 139-164.

Gergen, K. (1997). *Realities and relationships: Soundings in social construction.* Cambridge, MA: Harvard University Press.

Latour, B. (1987). *Science in action.* Cambridge, MA: Harvard University Press.

Nicotera, A. (1999). The woman academic as subject/object/self: Dismantling the illusion of duality. *Communication Theory, 9,* 430–464.

Prelli, L. J. (1989). *A rhetoric of science.* Columbia, SC: University of South Carolina Press.

Rorty, R. (1979). *Philosophy and the mirror of nature.* Princeton, NJ: Princeton University Press.

Rose, D. (1990). *Living the ethnographic life.* Newbury Park, CA: Sage.

Shotter, J. (1993). *Conversational realities: Constructing life through language.* Thousand Oaks, CA: Sage.

Van Maanen, J. (1988). *Tales of the field.* Chicago: University of Chicago Press.

8

The Challenge of
Writing the Critical/Cultural Essay

Clifford G. Christians

❖ ❖ ❖

Critical/cultural studies present an argument. Every article or book develops a thesis. Descriptive material without a critical frame is inappropriate. Therefore, the major-league challenge is getting the argument straight. Critical/cultural approaches crystallize. They bring ideas and data together and give them a trajectory. This writing phase of the interpretive process is central. Is the thesis clear and adequately documented? Is your analysis of the underlying issues esoteric and perfunctory, or illuminating? The credibility of the critical essay depends on its coin of the realm—the thesis. With the quality of the argument always in mind, reviewers and editors use the four major criteria described below in evaluating a critical/cultural manuscript.

❖ LOCATING YOUR WORK WITHIN AN INTELLECTUAL TRADITION

Superior manuscripts are explicit about their intellectual roots. Although the Frankfurt School first established the critical approach to social institutions and culture, significant bodies of critical/cultural scholarship have grown up alongside it. The considerable and intelligent literature in any of these subunits must invigorate your analysis. If you adopt an idiosyncratic voice and try to develop a case independent of these traditions, your essay will likely fail. *Critical/cultural* is an umbrella term for a number of different intellectual streams that overlap and intersect, but each has its own character too. The critical/cultural paradigm is not a set of distinct operations with clearly defined boundaries, but a montage of schools and trajectories. The veterans who edit journals and read papers take these approaches seriously; they tend to be jealous of the ideas and debates that characterize them. Therefore, to be reviewed favorably, your essay must demonstrate competence in the larger arena beyond its specific subject matter. Critical/cultural scholars have the double responsibility of knowing thoroughly both their intellectual roots and their particular research domain.

The sprawling field of critical/cultural studies can be organized around areas of scholarship with their own identity, such as the Frankfurt School, the political economy tradition, British cultural studies, pragmatism, Chicago School sociology, feminist cultural studies, rhetorical and literary criticism, and others. As you review the brief descriptions that follow, the question is whether or not your essay enriches the de- bates *pro* and *con* within these trajectories. If it floats disconnected from them, the intellectual location of your article will need to be specified and defended.

Some veteran scholars are able fruitfully to defy all given frames of reference, but most attempts at innovation only show a lack of rigor. They do not move the field forward, but typically reinvent the wheel instead. Cheap attacks and quick forays into a perceived problem are largely meaningless. Our academic task is making research and scholarship available for further debate and testing. This sharing of knowledge is advanced dramatically when it works creatively from established parameters.

Critical theory ordinarily refers to the Frankfurt School, which embodies an approach to cultural criticism developed by the Institute of Social Research at the University of Frankfurt beginning in the 1920s. With the devastation of World War I in the background, and postwar Germany in economic depression, the failed strikes and protests throughout central Europe called for an urgent reinterpretation of society and politics. In order to accomplish this, Max Horkheimer, Theodor Adorno, and Herbert Marcuse engaged classical German thought, especially Kant, Hegel, Marx, and Weber. They concentrated on the changing nature of capitalism and the contradictions between its rhetoric of equality and the forms of domination it nurtured. The Frankfurt School developed a distinctive style of criticism centered on the oppression of mass consciousness through the mechanisms of the commercial media. In spite of vicious disagreements among themselves on the details, they together saw the social sciences as caught in the "discourses and power relations of the social and historical contexts that produced them" and critical theory as a method of "freeing academic work from these forms of power" (Kincheloe & McLaren, 2000, p. 280). In its view, "mainstream research practices are generally" implicated in reproducing "systems of class, race and gender oppression" (Kincheloe & McLaren, 2000, ch. 5).

But the Frankfurt School from the 1920s to Habermas currently is only one critical tradition. The critical/institutional perspective of political economy has developed a substantial legacy as well. Political economists—Dallas Symthe, Herbert Schiller, Kaarle Nordenstreng, Armand Mattelart, and Robert McChesney, for example—critique "the role of transnational and domestic institutions as communications infrastructures and as manufacturers of public consciousness and self-consciousness" (Real, 1986, p. 463). Political economists "are engaged in uncovering the size, organization and influence of current media monopolies and cartels on the level of tangible history and economic data" (Real, 1986, p. 463). They concentrate on the ways that economic and political power control the processes of democratic decision making in the interests of the power holders. The conditions under which messages are produced and determined receive the emphasis, with a focus on changing the institutions and structures of production.

Cultural studies centered at the University of Birmingham operate on the level of ideological discourse. Since the 1960s and 1970s, a genre of scholarship under the title "cultural studies" has formed on the political character of knowledge production (cf. Nelson & Gaonkar, 1996). Rooted in the work of Raymond Williams and Richard Hoggart, British cultural studies has gained worldwide popularity through Stuart Hall's and Lawrence Grossberg's emphasis on culture and power (see Bennett, 1973; Grossberg, 1997; Sterne, 1999). Thinking politically about cultural and social life, writes Sterne (1999), "requires a theory of how things in the world are connected with one another"—that is, a theory of articulation —"based on the assertion that there are no necessary correspondences among different elements (people, ideologies, places, events)"; further-more, all cultural phenomena are articulated and must be understood in terms of their interrelations and configurations rather than as "free-float-ing ideologies, practices and constituencies" (p. 263).

Pragmatism and Chicago School sociology have anchored American cultural approaches to communications. James Carey revived John Dewey's fundamental insight that communication creates and sustains public life (Carey, 1988; Munson & Warren, 1997). Norman Denzin's (1992) interpretive interactionism redefines the symbolic interactionist tradition in terms of cultures. The media are at the center of the webs of meaning by which people understand and produce cultural forms. Com-munities are linguistic formations, with humans as narrative beings or-ganizing their experience through stories and conversation. In this social-constructionist view, symbolic systems create the reality in which we live rather than merely reflect it. The question for cultural studies in American terms is how a democratic republic can be constituted across a large continent in the face of industrialization, urbanization, and en-trenched individualism.

The critical tradition has a long history in Latin America (Biernatzki & Piñuel Raigada, 1995; Fox, 1988; Martin-Barbero, 1987; O'Connor, 1991), and critical/cultural studies are beginning to flourish in India and Aus-tralia. Rhetorical criticism (Lucaites, Condit, & Caudill, 1999) and literary criticism (Lynn, 1998) have developed powerful guidelines for analysis rooted in the liberal arts. Feminist cultural studies has established a sub-stantial body of research as well (cf. Mattelart, 1986; McRobbie, 1991, 1997; Press, 1991; Press & Cole 1999; Radway, 1984; Rakow, 1992; Reinharz, 1993; Siegfried, 1996; Treichler, 1999; Valdivia, 1995, 2000; Van Zoonen, 1994).

The attempt to develop a critical/cultural tradition has taken many forms and is known by varying labels in different countries: *les sciences humaine, Geisteswissenschaften,* critical theory, humanistic sociology, ethnomethodology, *la cultura popular,* interpretive social science, cultural hermeneutics, cultural science, and naturalistic inquiry. These names point to important differences in philosophical orientation, national tra-dition, research priorities, and ideological stances. Even though these dif-ferences are not sorted out here, they matter when doing research and publishing essays. There are basic agreements and an underlying logic within critical/cultural studies centered on the common assumption that the reality we experience is an ongoing social construction. Nevertheless, giving explicit recognition to the various traditions of this genre is crucial to successful publication.

❖ DISPLAYING SENSITIZED CONCEPTS

Establishing sensitized concepts is another important dimension of the critical/cultural essay. These are categories formulated from the research area itself, yet sufficiently powerful to explain large domains of social experience. This terminology takes its inspiration from Herbert Blumer's (1954) useful distinction between sensitizing and definitive concepts.

Quantitative research traditionally produces lawlike abstractions through fixed procedures designed to isolate concepts from the experience, attitudes, and language of the people being studied. IQ, for example, becomes the operational definition of intelligence. Sensitized concepts are a different device for ordering empirical instances. They generate an insightful picture and distinctively convey the meaning of a series of events. They strike gold; they get at the essence, the nub, the core, the heart of the matter. While they seek to capture the original meaning, they explicate that meaning on a level that gives the results maximum impact. Critical/cultural researchers identify with social meanings in their role as participants, and formulate seminal conclusions about them as observers.

Concepts are the gateway to the world, the point of reference by which critical interpretive research proceeds. If too vague, they hinder your coming to grips with salient issues; if wrongly formulated, they obstruct relevant problems from your investigation, thus fostering misunderstanding or leading to oversimplification. Science agrees on the significance of conceptual clarity and the need for fruitful interplay between theorizing and empirical data. The question here revolves around the nature of conceptualization itself, with critical/cultural research concerned with concepts that yield meaningful portraits, and not with statistically precise formulations derived from artificially fixed conditions. Sensitized concepts refer to an orientation short of formal definition, yet apropos enough to help us cultivate facts vigorously.

By sensitized concepts, we mean taxonomic systems that display an integrating scheme from within the data themselves. Whether by minting special metaphors, creating analogies, or using direct expressions, critical cultural research maps out territories through seminal ideas that become permanent intellectual contributions while they unveil the inner character of specific events or texts. A portrait, illustrative story, or analysis of ritual behavior that crystallizes sentiment and lifestyle—all such rhetorical devices are necessary for elaborating sensitized concepts. Examples of those well known in the literature are Cooley's "primary group," Ellul's "efficiency," Carey's "ritual versus transmission" view of communication, Tocqueville's "equalitarianism," Gramsci's "hegemony," Schudson's "capitalist realism" for advertising, McCarthy's "nonsynchrony," Rousseau's "noble savage," Kuhn's "paradigm," Veblen's "conspicuous consumption," Baudrillard's "simulacra," Innis's "monopoly of knowledge," Maslow's "self-actualizing," and Janis's "group think."'

Stressing sensitized concepts as the building blocks of qualitative research does not mean that you can settle for something intellectually immature. It simply takes seriously the fact that all human activity is interpretive. Sensitized concepts capture meaning at different levels and label them accordingly. We can peel the onion of reality down to different layers, depending on our purpose and expertise. By apprehending events at various stages of an ongoing centrifugal process, these cognitive frames suggest directions along which our inquiry should advance further.

From this perspective, research does not progress in a linear fashion, but moves in phases. Theorizing is sequential, with repeated observation necessary to clarify an emerging concept, which in turn improves the quality of further observation. Sensitized concepts must be continually tested, illustrated differently, and refined by further encounter with the situations they presume to cover. As impressions take conceptual form, they operate dialectically with the relevant literature. Accepted theories are always replaced with more illuminating and parsimonious ones, until all possible explanations are considered.

Social theory is not related to research methodology as physics is to engineering or microbiology is to medicine. The connection between intellectual work and field work cannot be understood in one-dimensional terms. Plato has convinced us apparently that if *B* depends on *A* for its existence, then *B* is inferior, and that generic knowledge is superior to particular knowledge. However, the *theoria-praxis* relationship is not linear but dialectical. For example, Florian Znaniecki's (1935, 1952) influential conception of theory, labeled "analytical induction," insists on generalizing from the data by abstraction rather than employing an inductive strategy based on counting instances. Znaniecki opposes causal explanations, because they assume that the formal purpose of lawlike statements is prediction and control. In a slightly modified version, grounded theory likewise integrates existential location with conceptual categories, emphasizing the integrative and interpretive character of theorizing without jettisoning natural settings (Glaser & Strauss, 1969).

Sensitized concepts arise from careful observation of phenomena and an in-depth reading of texts. Researchers identify with social meanings in their role as participants and formulate theory about them as observers. The best scholarship results from those who act simultaneously as members of the culture being studied and as trained anthropologists from another culture. Since the days of Plato, and certainly since Kant, we have recognized that experience alone is not the same as understanding experience. Quality manuscripts do not arise simply from personal involvement in the texts or situations under study. They show the capacity to make compelling generalizations. Critical interpretive research, in Norman Denzin's (1997) terms, takes ethnographic description only as a point of departure. It aims for viable social theory that itself is grounded in the language, definitions, and attitudes of those who are studied:

> Theory, writing, and ethnography are inseparable material practices. Together they create the conditions that locate the social inside the text. Hence, those who write culture also write theory. Also, those who write theory write culture. . . . There is a need for a reflexive form of writing that turns ethnographic and theoretical texts back onto each other. (p. xii).

Certainly, the general and specific always live in tension. Getting sensitized concepts appropriately focused is enormously difficult. Above all, conclusions must be returned to the concrete level for substantiation. A down-to-earth, everyday configuration must be the point of departure and constant touchstone as you pursue the judicious and systematic elaboration of enduring problems. In the process of weaving a tapestry, researchers attempt to reduce as much as possible the distance between the concepts of social science and those employed by the people being studied. Constantly moving between social theory and the immediate arena of human experience ensures that the conceptual indicators that are formulated will ring true on both levels; that is, they will be theoretically sound and realistic to the natives. However, concepts can be pushed beyond their range of application until they become commonplace or vacant. Critical/cultural scholars always stand in danger of their concepts becoming desensitized.

For Geertz (1973), the essential vocation of cultural studies is "to enlarge the universe of human discourse" and expand the horizons of human existence by making publicly available the manner in which others "have guarded their sheep," thus "enriching the consultable record" of what people have said and done (pp. 14, 30). Prophetic sensitizing concepts are the most lasting contribution critical/cultural studies can make. Manuscripts that show finesse, precision, and credibility with generalizations and conclusions will be published. Those that introduce sensitizing concepts to interpret and frame the issues will even be cited by others and will influence the field's scope and direction.

❖ EXHIBITING INTERNAL AND EXTERNAL VALIDITY

It is widely understood and accepted that field surveys and laboratory experiments must be externally and internally valid. Critical/cultural studies need to meet these criteria as well, though in terms consistent with their own assumptions. Objectivity is considered neither possible nor desirable. In this research perspective, fact cannot be separated from value; detached observation is unattainable. "There is no Archimedean point from which to remove oneself from the mutual understanding of social relations and human knowledge" (Rosaldo, 1989, p. 169). Disinterest and disengagement do not lead to quality understanding, but signify indifference. Maintaining a façade of neutrality disguises the researcher's motivations under the prestige of the white lab coat, and the supposition that research is value-free centers control in the hands of professionals and academics, who create a scientized agenda remote from everyday life.

Critical/cultural researchers confront that sequestering head-on; they work the backgrounds and sidewalks, but with *savoir faire* and competence. They aim at interpretive sufficiency. They polish their research and writing skills in terms of sophisticated interpretive practices— disciplined abstractions (John Lofland), coherent frames of reference (Alfred Schutz), triangulation (Denzin), ethnomethodology, thick description (Geertz), case studies, or discursive penetration (Anthony Giddens). In a fundamental sense, interpretive approaches are a temperament of mind—"the sociological imagination," as C. Wright Mills (1959) called it —rather than merely a series of techniques for handling the telephone, minicam, PowerBook, or interview pad. However, although the creative process always remains central, publishable essays demonstrate valid procedures and tough-minded standards (cf. Pauly, 1991). Critical/ cultural studies accept the maxim that research imprisoned within itself, and therefore self-validating, is unacceptable (cf. Clifford, 1988; Clifford & Marcus, 1986).

Forsaking the quest for statistical precision does not mean impreci-sion, but rather a rigor of a different sort. The principle of external validity compels naturalistic observers to be circumspect in generalizing to other situations. Have you (this guideline asks) selected the cases and illustra-tions that are representative of the class, social unit, tribe, or organiza-tion to which they properly belong? Cultural studies arise in natural settings, not contrived ones; therefore, the more densely textured your specifics, the more external validity is maintained. This concern is partic-ularly apropos in preparing case studies, a favorite qualitative tool be-cause it allows in-depth and holistic probing. Your goal is identifying representative cases rather than spectacular ones that are anecdotal and idiosyncratic.

Regarding internal validity, critical/cultural essays must reflect gen-uine features of the situation under study and not represent the aberra-tions or hurried conclusions of observer opinion. Culturalists are not interested only in gathering measurable details, such as mortality rates, but they disentangle the several layers of meaning inherent in all human activity. As Geertz (1973) puts it,

> What ethnographers are in fact faced with is a multiplicity of complex con-ceptual structures, many of them superimposed upon or knotted into one another, which are at once strange, irregular, and inexplicit, and which they must contrive somehow first to grasp and then to render. (p. 10).

There must be sympathetic immersion in the material until you estab-lish, in Blumer's (1954) phrase, "poetic resonance" with it. Do you know enough to identify the principal aspects of the event being studied and to distinguish these main features from digressions and parentheses? Using the body as an analogue, the blood and brain must be separated from fingernails and skin, all of which are parts of the whole organism but of differing significance. It is sometimes assumed that participatory observation can only serve an exploratory function, but critical/cultural research considers this a false assumption. If true interiority has occurred —that is, if data accurately reflect the natural circumstances—then the data are valid and reliable even though not based upon randomization, repeated and controlled observation, measurement, and statistical inference.

Qualitative studies start from the assumption that in studying humans we are examining a creative process whereby people produce and maintain forms of life and society, as well as systems of meaning and value. This creative activity is grounded in the ability to build cultural forms through symbols that express the will to live purposefully. The researcher's first obligation is getting inside the creative process, and the methodologies used must not reduce and dehumanize the area studied in the very act of studying it. Creativity is unique to the human species, and studies that are internally valid pay circumspect attention to this distinctive aspect of social life. People arbitrate their own presence in the world. Human beings are not puppets on a string, but live actors on a stage who improvise as the drama unfolds.

Humans live by interpretations. They do not merely react or respond, but rather live by interpreting experience through the agency of culture. This is as true of microscopic forms of human interaction (e.g., conversation and gatherings) as it is of the broadest human initiative (e.g., the attempt to build religious systems of ultimate meaning and significance). We are born into an intelligible and interpreted world, and we struggle to use these interpretations creatively for making sense of our lives and institutions. It is, then, to understanding the possibilities and contentions of human existence that critical/cultural studies are dedicated. The question is not, "How do the media affect us," but rather, "What are the interpretations of meaning and value created in the media and what is their relation to the rest of life?"

The guideline of internal validity is also paramount for the practice of exegesis, the reading of documents with depth and precision (cf. Lynn, 1998; Rapko, 1998). Failure on this expository level is especially debilitating, because the objective of critical/cultural research is rich detail. Ability to do accurate exegetical work requires cultivation so that a twitching eyelid is correctly interpreted as either a mischievous wink or incipient conspiracy (or simply a twitch). Admittedly, a developed textual sense can only be placed on a sliding scale from meager to rich, yet culturalists insist on it as an important axis separating competent from incompetent study. Too much cultural work appears with blurred categories and haphazard exegesis of documents. Authors whose manuscripts are accepted have distinguished literal from figurative, simile from allegory. They have established historical antecedents and origins, have discovered words in their social context, and know exact meanings of synonyms and parallels. Publishable material shows laborious attention to lexical details.

❖ WRESTLING WITH ISSUES OF SOCIAL ACTION

Scholarship in the critical/cultural mode generates social and cultural critique, leads to resistance, and seeks to empower readers to action. It shares a common aspiration: "to confront the injustice of a particular society or sphere within the society. . . thus becom[ing] a transformative endeavor unembarrassed by the label 'political'" (Kincheloe & McLaren, 2000, p. 140). A basic guideline for publishable research is whether it enables the humane transformation of the multiple spheres of community life—religion, politics, commerce, ethnicity, gender, education, and so forth. Critical/cultural studies do not reduce social issues to financial and administrative problems for politicians, but enable the public to come to terms with their everyday experience themselves. They value "writing that moves a public to meaningful judgment and meaningful action;" they exhibit a "form of textuality that turns citizens into readers and readers into persons who take democratic action in the world" (Denzin, 1997, p. 282). In Brian Fay's (1987) terms, critical social science seeks to provide "a much-needed impetus for the social and political changes which will have to take place if human life is to continue" (p. ix). The mission of your research is enabling institutions and public life to prosper. The aim is not fulsome data *per se*, but community transformation. Rather than research reports prepared for clients, funding agencies, or the academic apparatus, research is intended to be participatory in its execution, helping provide a forum for activating the polis mutually.

Power is considered a central notion in social analysis. Given its political-institutional bearing, oppressive power blocs and monopolies need the researcher's scrutiny in critical studies. However, economic, technological, and political systems in the best essays are not interpreted in cognitive terms only. The issue is how people can be empowered instead. In Paulo Freire's (1973, 1990) cultural terms, the meaning of power is reinvented:

> The radical transformation of society demands not getting power from those who have it, or merely to make some reforms, some changes in it. . . . The question is not just to take power but to reinvent it. That is, to create a different kind of power, to deny the need power has as if it were metaphysics. (Quoted in Evans, Evans, & Kennedy, 1987, p. 229).

In Freire's alternative, power does not aim at mastery, but ought to be understood in relational terms. Empowered persons are not distant and dominant, but are given their maximum humanity—power akin to Alcoholics Anonymous, in which vulnerability and exchange within a community enables persons to establish a sense of purpose and direction.

In the research process, power is unmasked and then engaged through solidarity with readers. The control version of power advocates manipulation if necessary, but the empowerment strategy seeks reciprocity instead of sovereignty. Rather than playing semantic games with power, critical/cultural scholars themselves are willing to march against the barricades. "Whereas traditional researchers cling to the guardrail of neutrality, critical researchers frequently announce their partnership in the struggle for a better world" (Kincheloe & McLaren, 2000, p. 140). Only when writers and readers fill their own civic space does empowerment mean something revolutionary.

In critical/cultural terms, power is not catalogued for its own sake but translated into strategies for change. The best essays argue for public policy and set agendas for citizen groups. Research on labor conditions in the workplace, for example, cannot simply produce "a catalog of incidents of worker exploitation," but must challenge "the assumptions upon which the cult of the expert and scientific management are based" and indicate avenues of "worker empowerment" (Kincheloe & McLaren, 2000, p. 150). In Arnold Pacey's terms (1992), critical/cultural research strengthens independent bodies operating in the public interest. It investigates the effectiveness and does research on behalf of Common Cause, Greenpeace, Friends of the Earth, World-Watch on Deforestation, the Stockholm International Peace Research Institute, and others. Mercedes Creel (1995) calls for support of alternative media production, such as those of the *Movimiento Feminista Manuela Ramos* in Peru. Robert McChesney's (1999) book on oligopoly, centralization, and monopolies in the global media concludes with a major chapter on political reform (pp. 281-319). In addition to his sociological analysis of alcoholism, Norman Denzin writes a book of implications and implementation for healthcare professionals. When James Carey (Munson & Warren, 1997) bemoans the paucity of public language and a public vision, he trades on Dewey's concern for developing a viable public philosophy. Carey argues for placing public justice at the center of our culture's institutional and organizational agendas. Schools, universities, park boards, county planning commissions, churches, healthcare watchdog groups, and the United Way are examined for public service, for evidence of strategic thinking and shared governance. The public theater is considered action space for taking initiatives, and critical/cultural researchers are both participants and interpreters.

The participation of the oppressed in directing cultural formation has been inspired especially by Latin American cultural studies. From this perspective, when important social issues need resolution, the most vulnerable will have to lead the way (cf. Gomes, 1989). Freire's reinvented power rejects the paternalistic, elitist view that the oppressed are powerless and must wait passively until the revolution is handed them. Third-world societies are typically considered cultures without agents. Their agency is ignored in the main dramas of capitalism, modernism, and imperialism that are played out among the main classes and interest groups in the self-proclaimed center countries. Even in well-meaning accounts of imperialism and colonialism radiating from Europe and North America, there is little recognition of resistance, indigenous struggles, and local alternatives. Non-Caucasians come through as dependent, with minimal talent and limited capacity for self-determining democracy. Therefore, critical/cultural studies that are mature and authentic go beyond monolithic abstractions of Western social theory to represent the voices of justice in children's theatre, aboriginal art, folktales, teen music, poetry, and people's radio (McCarthy, 1998, pp. 39-48). Revolutionary change, "which begins with the egoistic interests of the oppressor (an egoism cloaked in the false generosity of paternalism) and makes of the oppressed the objects of its humanitarianism, itself maintains and embodies oppression. It is an instrument of dehumanization" (Freire, 1990, p. 39).

Arrogant politicians—supported by a bevy of accountants, lawyers, economists, and social science researchers—trivialize the nonexpert's voice as irrelevant to the problem or its solution. However, transformative action from the inside out is impossible unless the oppressed are active participants rather than a leader's object. "Only power that springs from the weakness of the oppressed will be sufficiently strong to free both" (Freire, 1990, p. 28).

In Freire's (1973) terms, the goal is conscientization; that is, creating a critical consciousness that directs the ongoing flow of praxis and reflection in everyday life. In cultures of silence, the oppressor's language and way of being are fatalistically accepted without contradiction; however, a critical consciousness enables us to exercise the uniquely human capacity of "speaking a true word" (Freire, 1990, p. 75). Under conditions of sociopolitical control, "the vanquished are dispossessed of their word, their expressiveness, their culture" (Freire, 1990, p. 134). Rigoberta Menchú of the Quiche tribe in Guatemala won the Nobel Peace Prize in 1994; however, under conditions where "silence is gendered female," she "remains a token, for there are few if any others like her who get to voice their cause in global fora" (Valdivia, 2000, p.110). The voice she gains is only through "one of the colonial languages" (Spanish) and "is subsumed by news frames" that mention her "in passing as if to add color or tokenistic inclusion to stories about indigenous peoples" (Valdivia, 2000, pp. 120-122). "Those who have been denied their primordial right to speak their word must first reclaim and prevent the continuation of this dehumanizing aggression" (McLaren & Leonard, 1993, p. 17). Therefore, the fundamental challenge for critical/cultural scholarship is to foster conscientization—helping the oppressed gain their own voice and collaborate in their culture's transformation.

To serve as a catalyst for critical consciousness, your research must demonstrate that human lives are culturally complex and loaded with multiple interpretations. First-rate ethnographic accounts possess the "amount of depth, detail, emotionality, nuance, and coherence that will permit a critical consciousness to be formed by the reader. Such texts should also exhibit representational adequacy, including the absence of racial, class, and gender stereotyping" (Denzin, 1997, p. 283). Your research narratives ought to reflect these complexities and open up possibilities for social transformation in all their dynamic dimensions. Editors and manuscript reviewers expect critical/cultural essays to demonstrate this discursive power.

❖ CONCLUSION

It is often said that scholars do not produce their best work until six or seven years after their Ph.D. is completed. By then they have controlled their own agenda long enough and settled adequately into their own paradigm. If that conclusion is particularly apropos for book-length manuscripts, it implies for all scholarship that we let our research ferment and mature rather than rush it to publication. Clarifying the argument, getting the thesis straight, does not happen in a momentary flash of insight. Critical/cultural research is an interpretive process, and at various stages, illumination and ingenious ideas do help establish the argument and direction. Reaching the ideal of sensitized concepts, however, typically requires academic agony and ongoing struggle. If the article goes nowhere intellectually or the thesis in unclear, editors will reject it outright. At best, it will be given another chance through a major revision process. Developing a thesis that credibly and authentically interprets the event or circumstances or problem is audacious work. Quick and dirty studies, and those in a sophomoric tone, have no chance. If they do slip through a less-than-rigorous review, their publication will mar rather than enhance the author's career.

Guba and Lincoln (1994) argue that the issues in social science ultimately must be engaged at the worldview level. "Questions of method are secondary to questions of paradigm, which we define as the basic belief system or worldview that guides the investigator, not only in choices of method but in ontologically and epistemologically fundamental ways" (p. 105). How deeply critical/cultural researchers know their paradigm is, therefore, more crucial than knowing a dazzlingly array of methods. As with all social sciences, literature reviews are necessary to ensure that the research is novel or at least positioned well within the field as a whole. However, the critical/cultural model does not believe in descriptive literature reviews *per se*. The relevant documents must be evaluated, understood from the inside out, grasped in terms of assumptions and presuppositions. Nurturing a critical consciousness about one's worldview is finally the seedbed out of which excellent studies emerge. At work in our social science paradigms is a vision of life, and appropriating that vision reflexively is more crucial than implementing operational details. Knowing how the values and claims of the critical/cultural worldview are strengthened or contradicted in the literature is *sine qua non*. In this sense, writing well in this mode is tricky and often frustrating. You need to demonstrate to reviewers and readers that the relevant ideas, issues, and theories are accounted for and understood. Yet, to the degree the result is a scholastic exercise designed for true believers and advocates only, the mission of invigorating public discourse for social transformation is not fulfilled.

The critical/cultural paradigm is currently under development, and, if true to itself, will always be. Therefore, evaluation by reviewers will often be contradictory and sometimes appear to be arbitrary. Within a subunit, or from a narrow acquaintance with only one scholarly trajectory, your thesis may not appear to be well enough defended to one reviewer and pedantic or self-evident to another. Meanwhile, more generic journals, such as *Critical Studies in Mass Communications*, welcome the full range of critical perspectives, whereas others, such as *Cultural Studies, Media, Culture and Society*, or the *European Journal of Cultural Studies*, represent more limited traditions of critical/cultural research. Therefore, the overarching challenge in writing the critical/cultural essay is foundational—mastering intellectually a subunit within this paradigm and cultivating an understanding of its worldview. Those who are working the trenches will not be distracted by rejections, but will assess competently the evaluations *pro* and *con*. In the long run you will not be content with publishing a list of disconnected essays and reports, but will seek to contribute to the field's long-term development.

❖ REFERENCES

Bennett, T. (1973). Being "in the true" of cultural studies. *Southern Review, 26*(2), 217–238.

Biernatzki, W. E., & Piñuel Raigada, J. (1995). A Latin perspective on the media. *Communication Research Trends, 15*(3), 1–43.

Blumer, H. (1954, February). What is wrong with social theory? *American Sociological Review, 19*, pp. 3–10.

Carey, J. W. (1988). *Communication as culture: Essays on media and society*. Boston: Unwin Hyman.

Clifford, J. (1988). *The predicament of culture*. Cambridge, MA: Harvard University Press.

Clifford, J., & Marcus, G. E. (Eds.). (1986). *Writing culture: The poetics and politics of ethnography*. Berkeley, CA: University of California Press.

Creel, M. C. (1995). Women and men in Latin American media. *Communication Research Trends, 15*(3), 3–10.

Denzin, N. K. (1992). *Symbolic interaction and cultural studies*. London: Blackwell.

Denzin, N. K. (1997). *Interpretive ethnography: Ethnographic practices for the 21st century*. Thousand Oaks, CA: Sage.

Evans, A. F., Evans, R. A., & Kennedy, W. B. (1987). *Pedagogies for the non- poor.* Maryknoll, NY: Orbis.

Fay, B. (1987). *Critical social science: Liberation and its limits.* Ithaca, NY: Cornell University Press.

Fox, E. (Ed.). (1988). *Media and politics in Latin America: The struggle for democracy.* Newbury Park, CA: Sage.

Freire, P. (1973). *Education for critical consciousness.* New York: Seabury.

Freire, P. (1990). *Pedagogy of the oppressed.* New York: Continuum.

Geertz, C. (1973). *The interpretation of cultures.* New York: Basic Books.

Glaser, B. G., &. Strauss, A. L. (1967). *The discovery of grounded theory.* New York: Aldine.

Gomes, P. G. (1989). *Direito de ser: A ética de comunicacço na América Latina.* São Paulo, Brazil: Paulinas.

Grossberg, L. (1997). *Bringing it all back home: Essays on cultural studies.* Durham, NC: Duke University Press.

Guba, E. G., & Lincoln, Y. S. (1994). Competing paradigms in qualitative research. In N. K. Denzin & Y. S. Lincoln (Eds.), *Handbook of qualitative research* (1st ed., pp. 105–117). Thousand Oaks, CA: Sage.

Kincheloe, J. L., & McLaren, P. (2000). Rethinking critical theory and qualitative research. In N. K. Denzin & Y. S. Lincoln (Eds.), *Handbook of qualitative research* (2nd ed., pp. 279–313). Thousand Oaks, CA: Sage.

Lucaites, J. L., Condit, C. M., & Caudill, S. (Eds.). (1999). *Contemporary rhetorical theory: A reader.* New York: Guilford.

Lynn, S. (1998). *Texts and contexts: Writing about literature with critical theory* (2nd ed.). New York: Longman.

Martin-Barbero, J. (1987). *De los medios a las mediaciones: Communicación, cultura y, hegemonia* [*Communication, Culture and Hegemony: From the Media to Mediations*]. Mexico City: Gustavo Gili.

Mattelart, M. (1986). *Women, crisis and modernity.* London: Comedia.

McCarthy, C. (1998). *The uses of culture: Education and the limits of ethnic affiliation.* New York: Routledge.

McChesney, R. W. (1999). *Rich media, poor democracy: Communication politics in dubious times.* Urbana, IL: University of Illinois Press.

McLaren, P., & Leonard, P. (Eds.). (1993). *Paulo Freire: A critical encounter.* New York: Routledge.

McRobbie, A. (1991). *Feminism and youth culture.* Cambridge, MA: Unwin Hyman.

McRobbie, A. (1997). *Back to reality? Social experience and cultural studies.* Manchester, UK: Manchester University Press.

Mills, C. W. (1959). *The sociological imagination.* New York: Oxford University Press.

Munson, E. S., & Warren, C. A. (Eds.). (1997). *James Carey: A critical reader.* Minneapolis, MN: University of Minnesota Press.

Nelson, C., & Gaonkar, D. P. (Eds.). (1996). *Disciplinarity and dissent in cultural studies.* New York: Routledge.

O'Connor, A. (1991). The emergence of cultural studies in Latin America. *Critical Studies in Mass Communication, 8*(1), 60–73.

Pacey, A. (1992). *The culture of technology.* Cambridge, MA: MIT Press.

Pauly, J. J. (1991, February). A beginner's guide to doing qualitative research in mass communication. *Journalism Monographs*, No. 125.

Press, A. L. (1991). *Women watching television: Gender, class and generation in the American televison experience*. Philadelphia: University of Pennsylvania Press.

Press, A. L., & Cole, E. R. (1999). *Speaking of abortion: Television in the lives of women*. Chicago: University of Chicago Press.

Radway, J. (1984). *Reading the romance: Women, patriarchy and popular literature*. Chapel Hill, NC: University of North Carolina Press.

Rakow, L. (1992). *Women making meaning: New feminist directions in communication*. New York: Routledge.

Rapko, J. (1998). Review of *The power of dialogue*: Critical hermeneutics after Gadamer and Foucault. *Criticism, 40*(1), 133–138.

Real, M. (1986). Demythologizing media: Recent writings on critical and institutional theory. *Critical Studies in Mass Communication, 3*(4), 459–496.

Reinharz, S. (1993). *Social research methods: Feminist perspectives*. New York: Elsevier.

Rosaldo, R. (1989). *Culture and truth: The remaking of social analysis*. Boston: Beacon.

Siegfried, C. H. (1996). *Pragmatism and feminism: Reweaving the social fabric*. Chicago: University of Chicago Press.

Sterne, J. (1999). Thinking the Internet: Cultural studies versus the millennium. In S. Jones (Ed.), *Doing Internet research: Critical issues and methods for examining the net* (pp. 257–287). Thousand Oaks, CA: Sage.

Treichler, P. (1999). *How to have theory in an epidemic: Cultural chronicles of AIDS*. Durham, NC: Duke University Press.

Valdivia, A. N. (Ed.). (1995). *Feminism, multiculturalism, and the media: Global diversities*. Thousand Oaks, CA: Sage.

Valdivia, A. N. (2000). *A Latina in the land of Hollywood and other essays on media culture*. Tucson, AZ: University of Arizona Press.

Van Zoonen, L. (1994). *Feminist media studies*. London: Sage.

Znaniecki, F. (1935). *The method of sociology*. New York: Holt, Rinehart and Winston.

Znaniecki, F. (1952). *Cultural sciences*. Urbana, IL: University of Illinois Press.

9

The Challenge of
Writing the Historical Essay

Jean Folkerts

❖ ❖ ❖

Writing history successfully is a bit like being a good journalist. A historian must have a command of facts; be capable of creative, thorough, methodological research; be able to tell a story; and be aware of how his or her experiences influence the process. My goal in this chapter is to help historians become more successful in getting their work published regardless of their approach, methods, or topic. A good historical manuscript is one that moves beyond a banal approach to the creation of meaning by contextualizing the topic, applying interdisciplinary principles, grounding arguments in theory, and telling a good story.[1] I begin this chapter with a caution that you be aware of your approach to history and a reminder of the importance of communicating that to reviewers. Then, I turn our attention to a set of eight tasks that must be undertaken during the writing process. Reviewers are sensitive to how well you exhibit quality in the completion of this set of tasks.

❖   AWARENESS OF YOUR APPROACH

Historians are notorious for not making explicit their approach when writing a manuscript. Subtlety in such form no longer suffices and often serves to mask the fact that the historian has not thought adequately about choices made. Reviewers and editors instantly recognize a "fuzzy" approach. As a writer, you must make your choice explicit by discussing why you have chosen to address your research question(s) in a particular way. A reviewer of your manuscript should instantly know what approach you are taking.

Sometimes a writer of history may not be aware of his or her approach. Scholars who are trained in only one approach may not realize that there are alternative approaches. For example, some years ago, when I was an assistant professor striving to write research articles that would please the eyes of reviewers and editors, Donald Shaw, who was then an associate editor of *Journalism Quarterly,*wrote in one of his critiques that he appreciated my "American Studies approach." Until he wrote that comment, I had no idea I was taking an "American Studies" approach, even though my Ph.D. was in American Studies. Donald Shaw's comment has stayed with me over the years as I write manuscripts and read my own work as well as the work of others. It led me to understand that studying history was a process that emanated from a contextual state of mind. The context in which the historian found herself—time period, structure of society and education, for example—influenced the questions asked and the approach taken.

Approaches to media history are often confused with methods. However, there are important differences. Approaches are the lenses through which we view the world. Methods are the means we use to understand what is viewed through the lens. Understanding and articulating an approach enables the writer to choose the most appropriate method.

The choices of approach vary considerably, but they can be categorized into three major groups. The first is an American Studies approach, which focuses on American society as viewed through a cultural framework. This approach differs to some extent from the second approach, cultural/critical, which has emerged as a favorite choice in many disciplines, including English criticism and media studies. A third choice is empirical, which fits into a traditional mass communications exploration of theory and effects. These approaches may be combined to some extent, but each of the three clearly establishes a framework that is not merely descriptive in nature. All are interdisciplinary, combining elements of English criticism, American studies, anthropology, economics, sociology, psychology, and political science.

The American Studies Approach

The American Studies approach focuses on the interaction of individuals with culture and society. People are regarded as independent, powerful actors who are able to conceptualize for themselves. These actors participate within a cultural framework made of up societal institutions, and the focus of study is on the interaction.

Used to study media, this framework views communication as the foundation for developing a sense of community in a postindustrial world. Throughout the American experience, the development of media and media practice have been influenced by other aspects of the society. Consequently, this approach leads beyond a description of how prominent editors or publishers viewed themselves and focuses as well on working conditions of reporters, ad salespeople, columnists, and their relationships with the rest of the society, the characteristics of the audience, and economics.

An example of this approach is my study of Emporia, Kansas, editor William Allen White's desire during the latter part of the 19th century to use his newspaper to improve his community (Folkerts, 1983). In this article, I developed an explanation of White's efforts by looking at cultural values and norms through the theoretical structure of agenda-setting theory. I argued that White, and other editors of his time, structured the content of the newspaper through a choice of issues. With this theoretical underpinning, I argued that White, as a press leader in his state of Kansas, played a major role in disseminating themes of town growth, stable business politics, and preservation of a business power structure. White preached a philosophy of equal opportunity, and strove to maintain a stratified society with business control. Throughout, White was a strong actor who interacted with societal institutions.

Another excellent example of this approach is Carolyn Marvin's *When Old Technologies Were New: Thinking About Electric Communication in the Nineteenth Century* (1988). Marvin self-describes her account as a so-

cial history, in which "the focus of communication is shifted from the instrument [technology] to the drama in which existing groups perpetually
negotiate power, authority, representation, and knowledge with whatever resources are available" (p. 5).

Critical/Cultural Studies Approach

The critical/cultural studies approach to media history seeks, as does
the American Studies approach, to understand issues that are raised by
connections between media and society. Critical/cultural theorists look
at the symbolic meaning behind behavior and study the intersection of
media and everyday life, often focusing on the relationship of the media
text to its audience (Avery & Eason, 1991). However, the approaches differ in that critical/cultural scholars emphasize powerful institutions and
ideology.

This approach can be traced to Theodor Adorno, Herbert Marcuse,
and Max Horkheimer, theorists associated with the Institute for Social
Research in Frankfurt, Germany, who fled Hitler's fascist regime in 1933
and established themselves in New York with connections to Columbia
University. Scholars in the Frankfurt School did not believe modern media had the potential to improve society, but rather that they were "culture industries" that prohibited radical change and supported *status quo*
institutions.

Critical/cultural studies in the United States combines the ideas of
the Frankfurt School with an American approach represented during the
early part of the 20th century by University of Chicago scholars John
Dewey, Robert Park, and Charles Cooley, who focused on communication as a way of addressing a postindustrial world. These scholars act as a
bridge between the American Studies tradition and the Frankfurt School
approach. American scholar James Carey, who revived the community
orientation of American cultural studies in the 1960s and 1970s, argued
that communication should be viewed as a process through which a
shared culture is created, modified, and transformed. Communication,
writes Carey (1988), "is a symbolic process whereby reality is produced,
maintained, repaired, and transformed."

Steven Biel's (1998) study of reactions to the *Titanic* disaster provides
an interesting example of a critical/cultural approach to history. Biel cites

poetry and song that recorded responses by the working class, African Americans, and suffragists. This material clearly is a symbolic process incorporating the reactions of those who had little power to control their own worlds. Biel cites material from the opposition press that interpreted the *Titanic* disaster in ways far separated from conventional accounts, using content not to describe the transmission of information, but rather to describe how people interacted with an event to confront their own realities. Another good example of critical/cultural work is Carolyn Kitch's (1998) exploration of "The American Woman" series of illustrations that appeared in the mass-circulation *Ladies' Home Journal* in 1887. Her work underscores the illustrations as symbolic of communication as a cultural process, not as a transmission of information.

The Empirical Approach

The empirical approach is closely tied to the American tradition of communication studies, in which communication is viewed as a process of message transmission characterized by a variety of constraints and designed by professional communicators for either mass or specialized audiences. These historical studies focus on such factors as economic, political, and technological constraints. They often include serious examination of primary documents to uncover such accounts as the evolution of radio as an economic institution intertwined with developing technology. Although it is a common misconception that empirical studies are quantitative, they may involve a variety of methods. The word *empirical* translates to "experimental, observed, pragmatic, practical." Empirical studies include more traditional intellectual histories, quantitative studies of circulations (or the economics of publications or media industries), and studies of developing technologies. They are broad ranging and may include aspects of the approaches discussed earlier in this essay. The late Mary Ann Yodelis Smith (1981) captured the need for empiricism when she compared it to the mere collection and description of information. She wrote,

> Empirical history is merely the application of system and rigor to the study of the past.... [T]he impressionistic or scissors-and-paste historian industriously labors over notes about an event or person, shuffles them into topical

areas, adds the literary polish of transitional phrases, and tacks a summary at the end. (p. 306)

A classic example of empirical communication history is David Nord's (1988) article, "A Republican Literature: A Study of Magazine Reading and Readers in Late Eighteenth-Century New York." Nord was working in the rich archives of the American Antiquarian Society and discovered that a subscriber list was published in the first volume of the 1790 magazine, *The New-York Magazine; or, Literary Repository.* Nord investigated the people behind the names. Eighty percent of the subscribers lived in New York City, and Nord located 90 %, or 298, of the New Yorkers in city directories and other biographical sources. He found information on occupations and street addresses for 265. Then, he drew a random sample of 400 entries from the 1790 city directory. This sample gave him a basis for comparison that allowed for such conclusions as, "The readership of *New-York Magazine* was indeed more 'up-scale' than the general population of the city." Nord also read the 1790 volume and constructed a formal analysis of the content. By combining these techniques, he was able not only to describe the content of the 1790 volume and its subscribers, but also to define clear arguments. For example, he argued that *The New-York Magazine* was neither an "aristocratic literature accessible only to the elite" nor a "popular, democratic literature produced by or even directed toward the lower classes." But he understood that the readership was broader than previously thought, and that the content "affirmed the traditional values, while inviting all (except the truly poor) to take part. Like politics," the magazine "was an arena in which artisans and shopkeepers could participate in public life—in this case the cultural life—of the new nation." The magazine's content emphasized that participation, not social revolution, was the goal of artisan republicanism.

To write this article, David Nord (1988) had first to understand accepted truisms about colonial magazines. He had to recognize the significance of historical political concepts, such as "artisan republicanism," and that a relationship existed between journalism and political philosophy during the early republic. He explored a variety of sources and applied several methods. The beauty of this article is in the interweaving of the understanding of colonial political ideology and basic fact. Nord gave context and meaning to the existence of a single volume of the earliest of magazines. By using formal quantitative methods to analyze content, he gave credibility to his historical analysis.

❖ WRITING THE HISTORICAL MANUSCRIPT

Let us now suppose that you have constructed a historical project, gathered your evidence, developed your arguments, and are now ready to submit your work to a scholarly journal for publication consideration. At this point, you must shift your focus onto the reader. This is especially difficult to do if you have just finished a dissertation where your focus has been on your committee members and your purpose has been to demonstrate that you are capable of designing and completing a scholarly research project. Shifting focus onto the reader is also difficult for many well-established scholars who are very skilled at gathering historical data and perceiving patterns in masses of seemingly unrelated facts. However, even though the shifting of your focus onto the reader is difficult, it is essential if you are to be successful in getting your work published. What does it mean to shift focus onto the reader? Very simply it means getting inside the mind of the reader so that you can communicate your information in a sequence and pace that grabs the reader's interest, holds the reader's attention, and convinces the reader that your arguments are compelling. To help you shift focus onto the reader of scholarly articles, I address eight tasks below. The more skill you exhibit in addressing these eight tasks in your own writing, the more successful you will be in publishing your scholarly work.

Think About Theory

In writing history, you should make explicit connections to the existing body of theory. For example, in the piece mentioned above about William Allen White (Folkerts, 1983), I argued that his selection of news for the front page reflected agenda-setting theory. White had his own agenda, he placed news on the front page and highlighted information in the editorial columns in order to influence the public agenda. He persuaded editors who were his friends to publish similar information, then reported the appearance of such items as evidence that the "people" agreed with him. In other cases, the theoretical linkages may be less explicit. Theoretical statements sometimes take exception with popularly held views. "Revisionist" history reflects new interpretations of old material, sometimes causing a theoretical shift. Look at the following as an illustration.

In her article on New England colonial education and literacy, Jennifer Monaghan (1988) takes exception to the commonly held view that women were illiterate. She examines educational patterns in colonial America and discovers that women were educated, but they were taught to read, not to write. Writing was a skill associated with business functions not expected of women; nevertheless, women were expected to read because it was their duty and role to pass on information about religious and other behaviors. Because historians studying literacy had focused on who could sign his or her name, women had been declared illiterate. Monaghan challenged the existing assumption that women were illiterate. She then posited that literacy be defined in a different manner, and that consideration be given to the ability to read as well as to write.

Narrow the Project After a Thorough Literature Review

A dissertation is not a journal article. In writing an article, it is important to focus the topic more narrowly than in a dissertation. Let us suppose that you have decided to study 19th-century reform in relationship to the press. You determine that most of the work on reform has been confined to the New England states, but because you are interested in the Southern press, you have found, through reading, that Southerners advocated schools and colleges, the creation of libraries, changes in civil codes and prison conditions, improvement of public health facilities, and suffrage for women. Much of the discussion of social reform is recorded in period newspapers. You decide that you want to study antebellum reform in the South. You read widely in order to narrow the project.

The literature review is one of the most important sections of the study. It informs the questions you ask, the sources you use, the background you rely on. A literature review of a subject like the one discussed above should not confine itself to what has been written about newspapers and social reform. It should explore the entire literature of social reform and, in this case, of the Southern approach to reform issues. Before doing the actual research, the historian should have a full command of the literature relating to the period and to the issue.

As you read widely about social reform in the 1800s, you discover that one interesting aspect of studying reform is understanding the social vision newspapers had in regard to their city. Using Washington, D.C., as a sample case, you determine that, as the nation's capital, the city was gaining a certain social distinction as a southern city. At this point in your study, you have grounded yourself in the literature and begun to think about how to narrow your topic.

Elucidate Your Research Questions

These are the questions that guide your study. They direct you toward what it is that you want to learn. They should not be simple *how* and *why* questions. For example, a question such as "Did editors support reform?" opens only limited doors to intellectual inquiry. The questions should frame a debate and lead you to explore a variety of source material, to think in contextual ways, and to create the possibility for finding answers you do not at this point anticipate. In thinking about editors' social visions, such questions might be, How and to what extent did Washington newspaper editors concern themselves with reform issues? Did coverage/discussion vary with the political affiliation or social standing of the editor? Did reform issues reflect political party preference? Were editors committed to reform in Washington or only to reform of a national program? Did reform discussions reflect attitudes about class and race? What was the ideological nature of reform coverage? Did it, for example, reflect a desire to take care of the poor in the city? To create "morally correct" standards? To enhance the meaning of the democratic experiment? To create harmony between man and his environment?

Let us say that you decide that the goal of the study is to understand the relationship of Washington newspaper editors to their city in terms of local reform issues and city enhancement. Did editors identify with the city or were they simply a part of a national political community? These questions are derived from an understanding that the exercise of journalism is related to politics, to social class, and to attitudes about race. The questions also reflect an understanding of different types of moral reform movements in the 19th century. At times the emphasis was on making people be "good" or "morally correct." Other reform movements focused on such concepts as a harmonious life.

Articulate Your Methods

First, there is no such thing as the historical method. It does not exist. The writing of history, journalistic or otherwise, is an endeavor that uses a variety of methods, including the writing of biography and the use of economic analysis, social science statistical techniques, textual analysis, ethnography, and so on.

Traditional journalism history has relied on a variety of strategic analyses, as outlined by Yodelis Smith (1981) in Stempel and Westley's (1981) *Research Methods in Mass Communication,* a book that for some years held sway as the standard mass communications research text. She outlined these as *traditional documentary analysis* and *quantitative analysis.* However, since that time, journalism historians have become much more sophisticated about the various methodologies available to them, and editors examine manuscripts in terms of the methodologies used. For example, along with Yodelis Smith's more traditional documentary analysis, they look for methods including ethnographic research borrowed from anthropology and textual analysis, the basis for much of the research emanating from the country's English departments.

Similarly, quantitative analysis, which historians in some of the country's major Midwestern universities adopted from the social sciences, has become a useful tool in understanding the role of the newspaper in community settlement and in the business side of media. Carolyn Dyer (Smith & Dyer, 1992) broke new ground in journalism history with her economic analysis of antebellum Wisconsin newspaper ownership patterns, and others have followed her lead. Quantification in history, along with attention to formal theory, however, has created an enduring debate among all kinds of historians. In 1962, Carl Bridenbaugh admonished members of the conservative American Historical Association not to "worship at the shrine of that bitch-goddess, QUANTIFICATION" (Bridenbaugh, 1963, p. 326).[2] Nevertheless, Lee Benson's (1973) work on slavery and nativism and the disruption of political parties in 1850s New York, Stanley Parsons' 1963 use of multiple regression in electoral analysis, and Dykstra's (1983) grasp of social theory from reading the work of social scientists (which he incorporated in his study of *Cattle Towns*) paved the way for a new history, still anchored in the humanities but less wary of new analytical techniques and the application of theoretical structures.

The secret for choosing successful methodologies is in determining the question and recognizing the best method for addressing it. However, journalism historians cannot choose a course without adequate training in the methodology itself. Thus, Ph.D. training for journalism historians requires interdisciplinary approaches. No departments or schools of journalism maintain on their rosters of full-time faculty experts in social theory, ethnography, textual analysis, or the various statistical analyses that can be applied historically. Ph.D. candidates must work with the expertise of the entire faculty at the universities in which they are studying, not merely in the departments in which they are lodged. Adept editors will understand quite quickly whether an author is skilled at the methodology he or she is using.

That having been said, expertise in methodologies alone does not make a historian or create a successful manuscript. The choice of methodology should fit the task; however, a methodological decision should be accompanied by the kind of immersion characteristic of Yodelis Smith's (1981) concept of strategic analysis. It is the immersion in material, as well as the methodology, that characterizes long-lasting, significant works of history.

Jeffery Smith's (1988, 1999) beautifully precise works on printers and press freedom and intellectual inquiry in the early American period would have benefited little from quantitative analysis. He chooses a strategic-analysis method, brilliantly peeling the layers from the intellectual content produced by early editors and printers through extensive reading of texts. If you have read the preface of *Printers and Press Freedom* (1988) you will find that Jeffery Smith has read more colonial newspapers than most historians can imagine. It is his sense of intellectual inquiry coupled with his absolute diligence and immersion in the documents that leads Smith to the creation of literate and historically significant work.

Smith's (1988) comments, for example, on Thomas Paine's *The Rights of Man* and Paine's trial for sedition reveal an intimate knowledge not only of Paine's writings, but also of the writings of other prominent thinkers of the time period, such as Thomas Jefferson. It is the immersion in the work that allows Smith to write with great detail. For example, he notes that Paine did not attend his own trial, because he had gone to France to attend the Convention after the French Revolution, but that he was defended by Thomas Erskine, who emphasized the concept of a marketplace of ideas at the trial. Smith goes on to chronicle elements of the trial and its aftermath. The detail in Smith's writing is one key to his success as a historian.

Similarly, Richard Kielbowicz's (1986) discussion of the tensions of federal postal policy in the mid-1800s relies primarily on exhaustive examination of documents and a subsequent analysis. He is not content, however, to report the content of the documents, but rather ties it quite clearly to congressional arguments that emanate from attempts to protect certain interests. Such analysis requires immersion in the political, as well as journalistic, literature of the period.

Therein lies one of the keys to a successful manuscript submission— exhaustive work within the literature. Many historians believe that the need for such immersion works against the demand for a long list of publications on the *vitae*. However, editors instantly sense when an author's work is "thin," or not well grounded in the materials. Thus, each manuscript represents an enormous commitment of time. There are few data sets that can be used in historical work to "spin off" a number of articles.

The earlier example of studying reform in a Southern antebellum city provides the primary peg on which a decision is made about using quantitative versus qualitative methods. In order to generalize to a larger population, one must use quantitative methods. A quantitative analysis of Washington, D.C., newspapers will undoubtedly show limited attention to reform issues, and this method of analysis will allow you to generalize about treatment of reform issues in the period. Because you, in this case, used only Washington newspapers, you cannot generalize about Virginia newspapers or North Dakota newspapers, but you can intelligently discuss the Washington approach. Were you to use a sample of newspapers across the South, you could generalize to a greater extent. In fact, it might be wise to do so, and then to confine the qualitative work to a narrower region. However, to understand tone, depth, and emotionality of the response, qualitative work is essential. It is through the qualitative approach that we begin to understand the meaning of the conversation.

One of the mistakes qualitative historians sometimes make, however, is to neglect to discuss methodology. Historians should discuss the choice of sources and the use one makes of them. Underlying assumptions should be made clear and definitions should be operationalized. For example, one speaks of social reform in the earlier example. What exactly is "discussion of social reform"? It can be defined to include all references to treatment of the mentally ill, discussion of changes in the educational system, discussion of the penal code and/or penalties for disobeying laws, and all mention of giving women the vote. One writer might decide to exclude voting rights, however, arguing that this falls into a realm outside of "pure" social reform. Whatever the decisions, the rationale for making them should be clearly stated.

Scrutinize a Range of Sources

Editors almost instantaneously check for the range—the primary nature—of sources and the quality of understanding that accompanies interpretation. Traditional source material, as mentioned earlier, includes letters of editors and political figures, along with historical documents, such as the Constitution, the Bill of Rights, the Congressional Record, and newspapers. What scholars of the radical generation of the 1960s brought embarrassingly to light was that these documents cannot stand alone, and in some cases are actually suspect. The content of colonial newspapers, for example, may reflect more the image that an editor hoped to cast on his community than the reality of that community. The letters of editors and political figures were sometimes written simply to be saved. Or the sentiments expressed in these may have been generalized by historians to represent the thoughts and deeds of a larger public when, in reality, they represented the thoughts and deeds of people of a particular gender and class.

Historians, therefore, began to turn to new sources. Diaries became a source of information. When Joanna Stratton, working on a master's degree at Harvard, found diaries in her grandmother's attic, she was able to include in the annals of history the stories of women who crossed the plains. The story of western development was expanded from an account of economic expansion, political considerations, and agricultural development to a cultural account of the role of women in such expansion. Stratton's discovery became the source material for her thesis, and a subsequent book, *Pioneer Women* (1981).

Tax roles, city directories, newspaper records, diaries, maps, letters, period literature—scholars need to use all imaginable sources. Editors are particularly receptive to manuscripts that indicate a thorough search of such sources.

Contextualize Time and Place

To write history, one must be able to recognize place and time as factors that contribute significantly to the role of media in society. C. Vann Woodward (1986), a prominent historian of the South, in a slim volume titled *Thinking Back,* reflects how time, place, ideas, and audiences influenced the subjects he chose to write about and the questions he chose to ask. Woodward describes with great fervor his experience as a rather privileged undergraduate living in the South in the midst of the depression, and ascribes that experience to his decision to become a historian of the South. Place—his geographical place and his own place in time in Southern history—strongly influenced his life's work.

Many undergraduates of the 1960s who entered the academy in the 1970s and early 1980s recognized that their geographical places and their place in the continuum of history were legitimate forces in choosing topics for writing communications history. Until that time, journalism historians who chronicled the improvement of American journalism followed too uncritically the model set by early historians that all important journalism began in New York City and spread, in somewhat corrupted form, to smaller cities and more distant geographical locations. In doing so, they did not explore the contributions to communications history made by the various regions, ethnic groups, and small town editors who viewed their contributions far differently than did their New York counterparts.

One of the most understudied aspects of media history today is that of the foreign language press, a problem that results not merely because historians have chosen not to study the foreign language press, but at least partially from a lack of multilingual skills among historians. The archives of the foreign language press practically beg for attention. As our Ph.D. students and young scholars increasingly represent the multicultural nature of American society, the tendency to pursue the archives that document the past presence of different racial and ethnic traditions will likely increase.

Giving credence to one's place in the historical continuum leads to the asking of new questions. For those of us who were undergraduates in the 1960s, research as graduate students meant understanding confrontations with or challenges to the cultural and political order. The relationship of the nation's press and broadcasting systems to this cultural upheaval became topics for study. Daniel Hallin's (1986) view of the Vietnam War and Todd Gitlin's (1980) study of Students for a Democratic Society (SDS) and the media have significantly contributed to an understanding of media history. Increasing numbers of graduate students were black, female, working class—people with experiences different from those of the writers of the preceding generations. Many historians have written about the influence of these graduate student populations on the writing of social history—the incorporation of histories of working-class populations, of men and women who were not people of letters. This change is signified not only in the history of media producers, but also in questions about audience. The increasingly varied backgrounds of historians should lead to questions about the influence and role of mass media on audiences composed of ourselves—not on the loosely defined "other" or "mass" audience.

Woodward (1986) wrote that at an early point he recognized that what was needed in Southern history was to expose the fallacies, omissions, and long silences that characterized Southern history during the last half of the 19th century and the first half of the 20th. These silences included, he wrote, "the persistent themes of continuity and unity, particularly the continuity of the new order with the old and the unity of all whites through history." Such a focus led to the neglect of conflict between classes, races, and sections, and the "choral accompaniment of progress and prosperity, political conservatism, and sectional reconciliation" (p. 80). Such recognition by historians signal change in content of histories[3] (p. 94).

These recognitions have already lead a new generation of historians to ask a new set of questions. Events that occurred in the 1980s and 1990s generate new ideas. What does it mean when media become public companies, with stock to be traded and dividends to be paid? What does it mean organizationally? How does it affect the workforce? What are the forces in society that young scholars confront, both as scholars and as people, that drive their need to ask and answer questions?

Some writers address these issues straightforwardly. For example, in the introduction to *Gendered Lives: Communication, Gender and Culture* (1994), Julia Wood announces herself and discusses the personal why of her approach:

> This book reflects my belief that inequities are socially constructed and are harmful to all of us—those our culture defines as good as well as those it labels inferior. Three features distinguish this book and support the views I

discussed above. First, I include discussion of diverse classes, ethnicities, races, and sexual orientations whenever research is available. Unfortunately, what I can include is constrained by the limited study of people outside what our society designates as the norm. (p. 3)

Although Wood's work is not entirely historical, part of it is indeed, and she uses her own time and place within society to construct a cultural view.

Elizabeth Eisenstein (1983), who said she was influenced to write about communication as an agent of change in early modern Europe after reading Marshall McLuhan's *Gutenberg Galaxy* (1962), began to question the impact of the printing press introduced by Johann Gutenberg in the mid-1400s. She focused on the role of print in the Renaissance, the Reformation, and the Scientific Revolution, and found that the print shop "served as a kind of institute for activity . . . which rivaled the older university, court, and academy and which provided preachers and teachers with opportunities to pursue alternate careers." Eisenstein learned that the printing press allowed books to be treated as commodities, that merchants developed businesses selling books, and that these activities ultimately loosened the iron grip of the Catholic Church on the dissemination of information.

Eisenstein's (1983) work is a fascinating story that succeeds as a work of history because she respects the narrative style that makes history come alive and because she conveys an understanding of printing not only as a piece of technology, but also within the context of the society into which it is introduced. Further, Eisenstein gives her work relevance by conveying a tie both to the modern marketplace concept of media and to current inquiry about media expansion and influence in a global world. She maps the transition from a tightly controlled, narrow world to a world in which information became a commodity, and where increased numbers of ideas were distributed by merchants rather than scholars.

The historian's challenge is to make history relevant to the present day without invoking "presentism" that makes us interpret the past through the lens of a modern view. And although history "for the sake of history" is important, editors and reviewers will likely favor a manuscript that conveys relevance to today. Conveying such relevance often involves the contextualizing of time and place.

Tell a Good Story

Storytelling is a significant aspect of history. Young writers need to feel free to develop a narrative style that preserves the story, while at the same time basing the story on detailed source work. Writing a history is similar to writing works of literary journalism. You must adhere strictly to documented information, but you are free to express that information using the techniques of fiction that foster readability. Historians pride themselves on writing well, and an awkward account of good research will not suffice.

In telling the story, structure is important. The sections of the article should flow naturally. No matter what journal you select, you need to write a succinct introduction. Describe briefly what your research hopes to accomplish or what it is about. Think carefully: If you cannot capture in an introductory paragraph what you want to say, you have not thought about it clearly enough. Discuss research and methodology. Explain the variety of sources, the reasons for choosing the methodology and the approach taken. Make these explicit, then lay out the evidence so as to guide your reader to your conclusions. The argument, the depth of the evidence, and the clarity and logic of the evidence that leads to conclusions are the major tests of all historical work. These elements are the body of the manuscript. Conclusions must rest on a body of evidence, for the measure of a historian's credibility is in the evidence. Writing history is a bit like mapmaking: The historian's account is the map to the past.

Follow a Journal's Style Carefully

Journals employ their own official styles, such as *Chicago Manual of Style* (1983), with its many variations, or the Modern Language Association style book (Gibaldi, 1995). Be sure to adhere to the style of the journal. Some journals, such as *Journalism & Mass Communication Quarterly* (*JMCQ*), review manuscripts in a variety of styles and then require authors to conform the manuscript to style before publication. But beyond official style, journals have unofficial styles. Consult current issues of the journal carefully before submitting an article. As editor of *JMCQ*, I frequently have contributors asking whether their manuscript can exceed eleven pages—although the journal used to limit manuscripts to eleven pages, it has not done so for several years. Such inquiries offend editors, because they indicate clearly that an author has not read a current issue of the journal.

❖ CONCLUSION

This short guide was intended to help you write about the past and be successful in getting your scholarly writing published. To be a historian, you must be curious about the intricacies of policy making, of personalities, of why one decision was made when many alternatives were available. The past must ever enchant you. If you are to write history, the present must make you wonder what came before. This curiosity, coupled with a creative research-oriented mind, will take you beyond the narrow confines of a journalism history that simply chronicles events and people, and introduce you to a rich, contextual view of media as a societal institution. Such a combination of curiosity and discipline also will bring editors to your door and cause administrators to grant you tenure.

To be a historian is to face the challenge of thinking contextually, of going beyond description. Authors must interpret and analyze in ways that challenge their readers, and they must learn the value of journalism history framed by theoretical understanding of how people communicate. Successful historical writers will mine historical records with great diligence and will think theoretically. And then, they will tell us, the readers, a captivating, spellbinding story. They will, in fact, narrate to us a story of the past in a context that gives us understanding.

❖ NOTES

1. In the early 1980s, when Pamela J. Shoemaker and I were assistant professors at the University of Texas at Austin, we supervised masters and Ph.D. students who were writing theses and dissertations. We found ourselves explaining the "how-tos" so many times that we joined forces to outline an intelligent and efficient approach to writing a proposal. A condensed version of this document was published in *Journalism Educator* (Folkerts & Shoemaker, 1984).

2. Bridenbaugh delivered this address to the members of the AHA in December, 1962. Allan Bogue cites this in *Clio and the Bitch Goddess* (1983).

3. I first made this argument in relation to Woodward's work at an AJHA national conference in the late 1980s.

❖ REFERENCES

Avery, R. K., & Eason, D. (1991). *Critical perspectives on media and society*. New York: Guilford.

Benson, L. (1973). *The concept of Jacksonian democracy: New York as a test case*. Princeton, NJ: Princeton University Press.

Biel, S. (1998). Unknown and unsung: Contested meanings of the Titanic disaster. In J. P. Danky & W. A. Wiegand (Eds.), *Print culture in a diverse America* (pp. 203–222). Urbana, IL: University of Illinois Press.

Bogue, A. G. (1983). *Clio and the bitch goddess: Quantification in American political history*. Beverly Hills, CA: Sage.

Bridenbaugh, C. (1963). The great mutation. *American Historical Review, 68,* 326, pp. 313-331.

Carey, J. (1988). *Communication as culture: Essays on media and society*. Boston: Unwin Hyman.

Dykstra, R. R. (1983). *The cattle towns*. Lincoln: University of Nebraska Press.

Eisenstein, E. (1983). *The printing revolution in early modern Europe*. Cambridge, UK: Cambridge University Press.

Folkerts, J. (1983). William Allen White's anti-populist rhetoric as an agenda-setting technique. *Journalism Quarterly, 60*(1), 28–34.

Folkerts, J., & Shoemaker, P. (1984). Guide provides aid to students writing thesis proposals. *Journalism Educator, 39*(3), 30, 44.

Gibaldi, J. (1995). *Style manual and guide to scholarly publishing*. New York: Modern Language Association of America.

Gitlin, T. (1980). *The whole world is watching: Mass media in the making and the unmaking of the new left*. Berkeley, CA: University of California Press.

Hallin, D. C. (1986). *The "uncensored war": The media and Vietnam*. New York: Oxford University Press.

Kielbowicz, R. (1986). Modernization, communication policy, and the geopolitics of news, 1820–1860. *Critical Studies in Mass Communication, 3,* 21–35.

Kitch, C. (1998). The American woman series: Gender and class in The Ladies' Home Journal, 1897. *Journalism & Mass Communication Quarterly, 75*(2), 243-262.

Marvin, C. (1988). *When old technologies were new: Thinking about electric communication in the late nineteenth century*. Oxford: Oxford University.

McLuhan, M. (1962). *Gutenberg Galaxy: The Making of Typographic Man*. Toronto, Ontario: University of Toronto Press.

Monaghan, J. (1988). Literacy instruction in Colonial New England. *American Quarterly, 40,* pp. 18-41.

Nord, D. P. (1988, March). A republican literature: A study of magazine reading and readers in late-eighteenth century New York. *American Quarterly, 40,* p. 7.

Parsons, S. (1964). The populist context: Nebraska farmers and their antagonists, 1882-1895 (Doctoral dissertation, State University of Iowa, 1964).

Smith, C., & Dyer, C. (1992). Taking stock, placing orders: A historiographic essay on the business history of the newspaper. *Journalism Monographs* (No. 132). Columbia, SC: AEJMC.

Smith, J. (1988). *Printers and press freedom: The ideology of early American journalism*. New York: Oxford University Press.

Smith, J. (1999). *War and press freedom: The problem of prerogative power.* New York: Oxford University Press.

Stratton, J. (1981). *Pioneer women: Voices from the Kansas frontier.* New York: Simon & Schuster.

Wood, J. T. (1994). *Gendered lives: Communication, gender and culture.* Belmont, CA: Wadsworth.

Woodward, C. V. (1986). *Thinking back: The perils of writing history.* Baton Rouge, LA: Louisiana State University.

Yodelis Smith, M. A. (1981). The method of history. In G. H. Stempel, III, & B. H. Westley (Eds.), *Research methods in mass communication* (pp. 316-330). Englewood Cliffs, NJ: Prentice Hall.

Index

❖ ❖ ❖

About the Editors

❖ ❖ ❖

Alison Alexander is Professor and Head of the Department of Telecommunications at the Grady College of Journalism and Mass Communication at the University of Georgia. She was editor of the *Journal of Broadcasting & Electronic Media*, and is past president of the Association for Communication Administration and the Eastern Communication Association. Her work focuses on media and the family. She is the author of over 40 book chapters or journal articles, and the co-editor of three books. She was the 1998 International Radio and Television Society Frank Stanton Fellow.

W. James Potter is Professor in the Department of Communication Studies at University of California at Santa Barbara. He has served on the editorial boards of six journals, been a reviewer for a dozen more, and was editor of the *Journal of Broadcasting & Electronic Media*. Although he frequently has his work rejected, he has also had more than 100 manuscripts make it successfully through the peer-review process to be published in journals and presented at scholarly conferences. He has published six books on qualitative methodologies, media violence, theory, and literacy.

About the Authors

❖ ❖ ❖

James A. Anderson is Professor of Communication and Principal Investigator of the Rocky Mountain Humanities Center, University of Utah. He the author/co-author of 11 books, including *Communication Research: Issues and Methods, Mediated Communication: A Social Action Perspective, Communication Theory: Epistemological Foundations,* and *The Organizational Self and Ethical Conduct.* His 90+ chapters, articles, and research monographs are in the areas of family studies, cultural studies, media literacy, organizational studies, communicative ethics, methodology, and epistemology. He has been the editor of *Communication Yearbook, Communication Theory,* and Oxford University Press's electronic journal *Oxcomm,* Associate Editor of *Human Communication Research,* and has been a member of the editorial board of seven other journals.

Judee K. Burgoon is Professor of Communication and of Family Studies and Human Development, and Director for Human Communication Research for the Center for the Management of Information at the University of Arizona. She is the author of seven books and monographs and nearly 200 articles and chapters related to nonverbal and interpersonal communication and research methods, and is the recipient of the National Communication Association's Distinguished Scholar Award and the International Communication Association's Aubrey Fisher

Mentorship Award. Her editorial experience includes service as editor of *Communication Monographs* and serving as a member of 10 editorial boards, an invited reviewer for 15 other journals, and a panelist or reviewer for funding agencies.

Steven Chaffee is a professor and Rupe Chair in the Social Effects of Mass Communication at the University of California, Santa Barbara. A former newspaper reporter and editor, he has served as editor of *Communication Research,* and was founding editor of the *Communication Concepts* series for Sage Publications. He has edited several books, published more than two dozen synthesizing reviews as journal articles and book chapters, refereed book manuscripts for five publishing houses, and served on the editorial boards of *Journalism and Mass Communication Quarterly, Political Communication, Human Communication Research, Journalism and Mass Communication Monographs,* and *Public Opinion Quarterly.*

Clifford G. Christians is a research professor of communications at the University of Illinois at Urbana-Champaign, where he works with doctoral students as Director of the Ph.D. program in communications. He is the author, co-author, editor, or co-editor of seven books, and is the current editor of *The Ellul Forum.* In addition, he served a term as editor of *Critical Studies in Mass Communication,* has edited special issues for several journals, and is on the editorial boards of a dozen academic journals. He was a Pew Fellow in ethics at Oxford University, faculty member in the Pew Graduate Summer Seminar Program, and a Senior Mentor in the Pew Younger Scholars Program.

Jean Folkerts is Interim Dean of the Columbian College of Arts and Sciences and professor and director of the School of Media and Public Affairs at The George Washington University and editor of *Journalism & Mass Communication Quarterly.* She has worked as a daily newspaper reporter, a public relations professional and magazine editor for The Menninger Foundation, and a free-lance magazine article writer, and has served on the editorial boards of *Journalism Monographs* and *Journalism History.* She is a co-author of *Voices of A Nation: A History of the Mass Media in the United States* and *Media in Your Life,* along with articles about the nineteenth-century press.

Debra Lieberman is a communication researcher in the Institute for Social, Behavioral, and Economic Research at the University of California, Santa Barbara. Her research focuses on processes and effects of interactive media. Previously, she was an assistant professor in the Department of Telecommunications at Indiana University, Bloomington, and was vice president of research at two software companies that produce interactive media for health behavior change. She has published 12 comprehensive synthesizing reviews and more than 100 literature reviews within research articles, book chapters, conference papers, research reports, and grant proposals.

Thomas R. Lindlof is a professor in the School of Journalism and Telecommunications at the University of Kentucky, and editor of *The Journal of Broadcasting & Electronic Media.* His research interests include media audience theory and research, cultural politics, and the methodology of cultural hermeneutics. Lindlof has published widely in communication journals and edited volumes, edited and authored several other books, and served as referee for many journals in communication, consumer behavior, geography, and psychology. Currently, he is a member of the editorial boards of *Mass Communication and Society* and *The Journal of Media and Religion,* and previously served on the boards of *Human Communication Research* and *The Journal of Broadcasting & Electronic Media.*

Alan M. Rubin is Professor and Interim Director of the School of Communication Studies at Kent State University. His research interests include media uses and effects, the interface of personal and mediated communication, and newer communication technologies. He is a past editor of the *Journal of Broadcasting & Electronic Media* and the *Journal of Communication.*

Printed in the United States
121227LV00002BC/3/P